THE PREPARED PROPHET

.

THE PREPARED PROPHET

TONY MEDLEY

MEDLEY

Contents

Published by Medley Publishing Group
Printed in the United States of America

ISBN (Paperback): 979-8-9940033-1-2
ISBN (eBook): 979-8-9940033-2-9

Cover design and interior layout by Tory Medley

Scripture quotations are taken from the Holy Bible ,King James Version®, unless otherwise noted. All emphasis within Scripture quotations (italics, bold, capitalization) has been added by the author.

This book is not intended to replace personal study of Scripture or spiritual counsel, but to serve as a resource for spiritual development, reflection, and biblical growth.

The author and publisher do not assume responsibility for any actions taken by readers based on the content of this book. Readers are encouraged to seek prayer, discernment, and spiritual counsel as appropriate.
First Edition, 2025

Dedicated to every hidden vessel, every obedient heart, and every surrendered soul standing quietly in the shadow of God's greatness.
To the prophets who wrestle with calling in the midnight hours...
To those who feel God's burden but have no one to share it with...
To those who hear Heaven's whisper while the world sleeps...
To those who have been crushed, refined, shaped, stripped, rebuilt, and recommissioned...
This book is for you.
And finally, to Jesus Christ—the Author, the Revealer, the Redeemer, and the One true Voice behind every prophetic voice.
May every page draw you deeper into His presence.

Preface

The Prepared Prophet was birthed from a deep conviction that God is raising a new generation of prophetic vessels—men and women who long not for platforms, applause, or spectacle, but for purity, intimacy, and authentic partnership with Heaven.

Over the years, prophetic ministry has been misunderstood, misused, sensationalized, or reduced to displays of gifting rather than expressions of God's heart. But Scripture reveals a far more sacred reality: true prophets are not defined by their abilities, but by their closeness to God. They are shaped through process, refined through suffering, trained through intimacy, and commissioned through surrender.

This book is not an academic exploration of prophecy, nor merely a manual on prophetic gifting—it is a journey through the inner life of the prophet. It is a roadmap through calling, struggle, breaking, redeeming, and commissioning. It is a guide for those who sense that God is tugging them deeper but cannot fully articulate the stirring within their spirit.

Every chapter was written with prayer, intentionality, and a desire to restore honor and clarity to prophetic ministry. If you read these pages with an open heart, I believe the Holy Spirit will cultivate within you the same depth of hunger and consecration that has guided prophetic vessels since the days of Enoch, Jeremiah, Ezekiel, and Isaiah.

May this book not only teach you but transform you.
May it not merely inform you but shape you.

And may every word point you toward the One who is the center of all prophecy—

Jesus Christ, the living Word of God.

—DR. TONY E. MEDLEY SR. , MEDLEY PUBLISH-
ING GROUP

Introduction

The prophetic calling is unlike any other. It is glorious, yet costly. Beautiful, yet weighty. Profound, yet humbling. Prophets stand at the intersection of Heaven and earth—listening to God while standing among humanity, receiving divine messages yet carrying fragile emotions, seeing deeply yet often walking alone.

Many desire prophetic power, yet few understand prophetic formation. Before God gives a prophet a voice to the nations, He gives them a wilderness. Before He gives them a platform, He gives them a process. Before He hands them revelation, He hands them refinement.

This book explores that sacred formation.

Prophets are shaped differently. They feel differently. They see differently. They walk differently. They wrestle with things others cannot perceive. They carry burdens others never feel. They are misunderstood, resisted, sometimes rejected, yet ultimately used as instruments of God's mercy, justice, warning, and redemption.

The Prepared Prophet exists to make sense of that journey.
To encourage those who feel unusual.
To strengthen those who feel isolated.
To clarify those who feel called but unprepared.
To guide those wrestling with a mantle they did not choose but cannot escape.

If you feel drawn to the prophetic...
If you feel God tugging you into deeper waters...
If you feel set apart without knowing why...

If you have endured crushing, stripping, loneliness, and spiritual burden...

Then this book is your companion.

You are not strange.
You are not broken.
You are not lost.
You are being prepared.

And the God who began the work in you will finish it,
fashioning you into a prophet who carries His heart faithfully into the earth.

1

The God Who Still Speaks

Rediscovering the Prophetic Voice Today

INTRODUCTION: A SILENT GENERATION IN A SPEAKING GOD'S WORLD

We live in an age saturated with sound—notifications, opinions, alerts, entertainment, and endless information. Yet for all the noise, one thing remains tragically rare: the clear, unadulterated voice of God. The modern believer is often overfed with content but undernourished by revelation. Many Christians hear sermons every week, but few perceive the whisper of the Spirit. Many attend church faithfully, but few have cultivated the spiritual sensitivity necessary to discern when God is speaking directly to their spirit.

Yet the Scriptures paint a different picture—one of a God who speaks, who leads, who reveals, who warns, who comforts, who directs, and who empowers His people by His voice. From Genesis to Revelation, God never ceased speaking. What changed was not His willingness to speak, but humanity's willingness to listen.

Prophets, throughout the biblical narrative, were not extraordinary because they possessed superior spirituality. They were extraordinary because they possessed superior availability. They made room for the voice of God in a world that constantly tries to silence it. They trained their ears to recognize heavenly frequencies. They positioned their lives like antennas aimed toward the throne room. They were lightning rods for divine communication.

The Prepared Prophet is not simply someone who can prophesy. The prepared prophet is someone who can perceive—someone whose life is aligned to hear God clearly and respond boldly to what He says. This first chapter lays the foundation: rediscovering a God who has not gone mute, who still speaks to His children, and who is raising a prophetic people prepared to hear Him in this hour.

1. THE CONTINUITY OF A SPEAKING GOD

If we strip human history down to its core, we discover a simple truth: God has always chosen relationship over silence. From the very beginning, God walked with Adam in the cool of the day. Their fellowship was not built on ritual but on communication. God conversed with Noah, directing him to build an ark. He spoke to Abraham, calling him out of Ur and into destiny. He spoke to Moses from a burning bush and again on a mountain engulfed in glory. He spoke to Samuel as a child, to David as a shepherd and king, to Elijah in a still small voice, to Jeremiah in youth, and to Ezekiel in visions.

The testimony of Scripture is undeniable: every generation had access to God's voice. The question is not whether God still speaks. The question is whether His people still posture themselves to hear Him.

God is unchanging in His eternal nature. If He spoke then, He speaks now. Jesus described Himself as the Shepherd whose sheep "hear His voice," implying not only the Shepherd's speech but the sheep's ability to discern it. The Holy Spirit was poured out on all flesh—not to silence prophecy, but to multiply it through dreams, visions, and supernatural guidance.

Divine communication is not reserved for spiritual elites. It is the inheritance of every believer. Yet prophets serve a unique function within this inheritance: they model what it looks like to have a life fully yielded to divine direction.

2. WHY THE PROPHETIC VOICE IS NEEDED NOW MORE THAN EVER

The prophetic voice is not optional in the modern world—it is essential. We are living in days of global instability, moral confusion, rapid cultural shifts, and spiritual conflict that is intensifying. When chaos increases, prophetic clarity becomes crucial. When deception abounds, discernment becomes vital.

We need prophets—not merely individuals who carry titles, but men and women who carry the burden of the Lord. Prophets who speak with conviction, purity, humility, and boldness. Prophets who carry both truth and love. Prophets who discern not only what God is saying, but why He is saying it.

Why is the prophetic so crucial today?

1. **Because deception is increasing.** People mistake their emotions for divine revelation. Many follow charismatic personalities instead of the Holy Spirit. Without a renewed prophetic standard, the line between God's voice and human imagination becomes blurred.

2. **Because God still has instructions for His people.** He gives direction before decisions, warnings before judgment, encouragement before endurance, and vision before victory.

3. **Because the church must be equipped for relevance.** Without prophetic insight, churches repeat routines without revelation. They operate by programs instead of presence.
4. **Because nations rise and fall based on prophetic obedience.** Throughout history, God used prophets to warn kings, redirect nations, and call people back to Himself. Prophetic clarity has national impact.

We are standing in a moment where God is calling forth a generation of prepared prophets—those who will not treat the prophetic as a tool but as a stewardship.

3. THE PROBLEM: MANY HEAR BUT FEW LISTEN

One of the most overlooked truths in the prophetic realm is this: God is always speaking, but we are not always listening. Many believers approach God with monologues instead of dialogue. Prayer becomes an endless list of needs instead of a place of communion. The modern Christian is often busy in ministry but barren in intimacy.

Many desire the gift of prophecy but neglect the discipline of listening.

What prevents people from hearing God clearly?

A. **Noise.** The enemy does not have to silence you; he only needs to distract you. The competition for your attention is relentless. Spiritual sensitivity dies when the soul is overloaded.
B. **Unbelief.** Many subconsciously believe God does not speak anymore. Others assume hearing from God is for leaders, not everyday believers.
C. **Sin and disobedience.** Nothing muffles the voice of the Spirit like willful sin. Prophets are not perfect, but they are repentant.

D. **Impatience.** God's voice is not microwaved. He often speaks in stillness, and modern believers rarely pause long enough to receive.

E. **Busyness.** Activity is not productivity in the Spirit. Many do more for God than they do with God.

The prepared prophet confronts these obstacles, rearranging life so that God's voice is not an interruption but the foundation.

4. GOD SPEAKS IN DIFFERENT WAYS, BUT ALWAYS CONSISTENTLY WITH SCRIPTURE

The prophet must understand that God is not limited in method, but He is consistent in principle. His voice will never contradict His Word. His Spirit will never approve what His Scripture condemns. His guidance is always aligned with His character.

God speaks through:

- The inward witness. A gentle prompting, an inner knowing, a divine nudge.
- The written Word. The ultimate standard for confirming revelation.
- The voice of the Holy Spirit. Sometimes gentle, sometimes forceful, always clear to the discerning.
- Dreams and visions. Symbolic, instructive, and often directional.
- Prophetic impressions. A burden, a warning, an insight into unseen realities.
- Circumstances. Closed and open doors, divine timing, providential alignment.
- Godly counsel. Prophets are trained in solitude but confirmed in community.

The prepared prophet learns to recognize these channels—not chasing supernatural experiences, but cultivating supernatural sensitivity.

5. THE NECESSITY OF A LIFESTYLE PREPARED FOR REVELATION

Prophetic gifting is not enough. Many have prophetic ability, but few cultivate prophetic maturity. Spiritual gifting without spiritual grounding produces instability. Revelation without preparation breeds arrogance or error.

So what prepares a prophet?

A. **A consecrated life.** Prophets live differently because they hear differently. Purity amplifies clarity. Holiness sharpens discernment.

B. **A disciplined prayer life.** Prophets do not pray to check a box—they pray to stay connected.

C. **A surrendered will.** God will not speak deeply to those who refuse to obey quickly.

D. **A teachable spirit.** Prophets must be trained, corrected, sharpened, and held accountable.

E. **A cultivated stillness.** Revelation comes to rest, not to restlessness.

A prepared prophet builds a lifestyle that God can trust with divine secrets.

6. THE PROPHETIC BURDEN: WHAT GOD SPEAKS, HE ENTRUSTS

Hearing God is not casual—it is covenantal. When God speaks, He entrusts. When He reveals, He requires responsibility. Prophets are watchmen, guardians of divine communication. They must steward what they hear with faithfulness.

A prophetic word is not a spiritual decoration—it is a spiritual delegation. God entrusts prophets with His heart for people, His warnings for nations, His encouragement for the weary, His direction for His church.

With revelation comes responsibility.
With responsibility comes weight.
With weight comes preparation.

This book exists to prepare you for that weight.

7. GOD'S VOICE AWAKENS IDENTITY

Every prophet in Scripture was transformed not simply by hearing God—but by being defined through what God said about them. Identity precedes assignment.

God called Abraham a father before he had children.
He called Gideon a mighty warrior while hiding in fear.
He called Jeremiah a prophet while he was a youth.
He called Peter a rock while he was unstable.

Prophets learn who they are by listening to who He is.

The prepared prophet must understand:
Your calling is not discovered by looking at yourself but by listening to God.

The voice of God awakens identity, and identity fuels destiny.

8. THE PROPHETIC VOICE IS NOT ABOUT PREDICTION—IT'S ABOUT ALIGNMENT

Modern culture often associates prophecy with predicting the future. But biblical prophecy has a deeper purpose: alignment. Prophets bring God's people into alignment with His will, His word, and His ways.

Prophecy is not fortune-telling.
It is divine alignment.
It is heavenly perspective.
It is God's will made visible.

Sometimes God speaks to reveal what will happen.
More often, He speaks to reveal what should happen.

The prepared prophet becomes a conduit of divine alignment.

9. THE CALL TO PROPHETIC MATURITY

Prophetic gifting without maturity is dangerous. Many people can sense things spiritually, but sensing without stewardship leads to confusion. Accuracy without character leads to corruption. Revelation without humility leads to manipulation.

Mature prophets:

- test what they hear
- seek the Holy Spirit's timing
- submit to spiritual authority
- speak with love

- avoid spiritual pride
- communicate with wisdom

A prepared prophet is committed not just to gifting, but to growth.

10. A PROPHETIC GENERATION IS RISING

In this generation, God is awakening prophetic sensitivity on a scale not seen in decades. Young and old alike are dreaming prophetic dreams. Believers are experiencing supernatural insight. Churches are being stirred with fresh hunger for the Spirit's voice.

This is not accidental.
This is intentional.
God is preparing a prophetic generation—not for entertainment or spiritual theatrics, but for Kingdom advancement.

We are entering a moment where:

- prophetic clarity will expose hidden agendas
- prophetic courage will confront injustice
- prophetic integrity will restore credibility
- prophetic obedience will shift spiritual atmospheres
- prophetic intercession will avert crises
- prophetic voices will awaken revival

God is speaking again—and He is preparing prophets who will not compromise His voice.

11. THE COST OF HEARING GOD

Before any prophet embraces the privilege of hearing God, they must confront the price of hearing God. Revelation is costly. God reveals Himself to those who are willing to be consumed by what He reveals.

Prophets carry a burden others do not understand.
They see what others ignore.
They hear what others dismiss.
They feel what others overlook.
They speak when others remain silent.

Hearing God requires:

- sacrifice
- separation
- sensitivity
- surrender
- spiritual formation

The prepared prophet accepts the cost because the presence of God is worth more than the approval of people.

12. A DECLARATION FOR THE PREPARED PROPHET

As we conclude this opening chapter, let this declaration mark your spirit:

"Lord, prepare my ears to hear You,
my heart to receive You,
my life to obey You,
and my spirit to discern You.

Make me a prepared prophet—
faithful, yielded, bold, and pure."

This is the beginning of your prophetic journey.

2

The Weight of the Call

Understanding Prophetic Identity

INTRODUCTION: WHEN GOD INTERRUPTS A LIFE

Every prophet's journey begins the same way: with an interruption.

God disrupts the ordinary. He invades the plan. He pierces through the routine with a summons that cannot be ignored. The prophetic life does not start with ambition or desire; it starts with divine initiative. God chooses the moment, the messenger, and the mission.

The call to prophetic ministry is not casual—it is costly. It is not glamorous—it is sobering. It is not about a platform—it is about a burden. The true prophetic calling demands maturity, courage, resilience, and surrender. It requires a willingness to stand alone, to speak truth when truth is unpopular, to hear God when silence seems easier, and to obey Him even when obedience disrupts your comfort.

This chapter explores the weight of that divine calling—the identity, the process, the burden, and the responsibility of becoming a prophet who is truly prepared.

1. THE CALL IS A REVELATION, NOT AN AMBITION

No one in Scripture ever volunteered to be a prophet.
Moses resisted.
Jeremiah protested.
Jonah ran.
Isaiah trembled.
Ezekiel fell on his face.
Amos insisted he was not qualified.
Elisha burned his livelihood to obey.

The prophetic calling is not a career—it's a consecration. It is not something a person decides to pursue; it is something God decides to reveal. It is a heavenly summons that demands earthly surrender.

Many today seek prophetic titles without prophetic transformation. They desire recognition without responsibility, influence without intimacy, and gifting without grounding. But the prepared prophet understands:

You do not choose the call.
The call chooses you.

The prophetic mantle is revealed through:

- divine encounter
- inner conviction
- spiritual awakening
- repeated confirmation
- undeniable burden
- God's sovereign choosing

And once the call is revealed, life is never the same.

2. THE CALL CONFRONTS IDENTITY BEFORE IT RELEASES ASSIGNMENT

Before God entrusts a prophet with a message, He confronts their identity.

Before the prophet speaks to others, God speaks to the prophet.

Before the prophet delivers the word, God delivers the prophet.

Every biblical prophet had to be transformed before they could be trusted.

Moses had to confront his insecurity.
He saw only his weaknesses; God saw his assignment.

Jeremiah had to confront his youthfulness.
He believed he was too young; God believed he was chosen.

Isaiah had to confront his unclean lips.
He felt unworthy; God purified his purpose.

Gideon had to confront his fear.
He saw himself as insignificant; God saw him as a warrior.

Peter had to confront his instability.
He was impulsive; God shaped him into a foundation.

Identity is the first battleground of the prophetic.
God does not begin with your ministry—He begins with you.

He calls you:

- before you feel ready
- before you feel worthy
- before you feel capable

• before you feel qualified

Why?

Because prophets are shaped by calling, not credentials. Purpose births identity, not the other way around.

3. THE CALL AWAKENS A BURDEN FOR THE HEART OF GOD

Prophecy is not about predicting events—it's about carrying God's heart. The true hallmark of a prophet is burden. They feel what God feels. They carry what God carries. They perceive the unseen struggles of others, the spiritual climate of a region, the condition of the church, and the urgency of divine timing.

The prophetic burden is not emotional—it is spiritual. It comes as:

- a weight
- a stirring
- a conviction
- a sense of urgency
- a deep compassion
- a holy dissatisfaction
- a longing for alignment with God's will

Prophets weep over what God weeps over.

They rejoice over what God rejoices over.

They stand in the gap when others stand aside.

A prophetic calling is not proven by how loudly you speak, but by how deeply you feel. Before a prophet declares "Thus says the Lord," they often whisper, "Lord, break my heart for what breaks Yours."

4. THE CALL SEPARATES BEFORE IT ELEVATES

The prophetic path is not crowded. It is narrow, sacred, and often lonely. The call separates you long before it elevates you. God will often pull a prophet away from:

- familiar environments
- unfruitful relationships
- spiritual noise
- unhealthy influences
- ordinary pursuits
- the comfort of complacency

Why?

Because prophetic clarity requires prophetic consecration.
The prepared prophet must learn to be comfortable with isolation.

This separation is not rejection—it is refinement.
God teaches prophets in caves, deserts, and wildernesses.
He develops them in hidden places before He reveals them in public spaces.

The separation season teaches:

- humility
- dependency on God
- sensitivity to the Spirit
- discernment
- inner strength
- spiritual endurance
- the discipline of stillness

Every prophet must embrace the season of being set apart. Without separation, there is no revelation. Without revelation, there is no prophetic authority.

5. THE CALL REQUIRES SURRENDER, NOT SUPERIORITY

Prophets are not called because they are better—they are called because they are surrendered

The prophetic calling does not create arrogance—it crushes it

The weight of hearing God humbles the prophet.

A true prophet understands:

- God's voice is sacred
- obedience is non-negotiable
- revelation is stewardship
- titles mean nothing
- posture means everything

The prepared prophet does not seek to be impressive—they seek to be obedient. They understand that the prophetic mantle is a privilege, not a pedestal.

Here is the sober truth:

God uses broken vessels, but He does not use proud ones.

Prophetic identity must be rooted in humility and holiness, not comparison or competition.

6. THE CALL IS CONFIRMED THROUGH PROCESS

A prophetic calling is not established in a moment—it is confirmed over time.

Many receive glimpses of their calling, but few endure the process required to walk in it.

The prophetic process includes:

A. **Training.** Prophets must learn Scripture, spiritual principles, and the ways of God.
B. **Testing.** Purity of motive must be proven. Character must mature. Discernment must sharpen.
C. **Correction.** Prophets must be teachable and accountable. Correction is not punishment—it is protection.
D. **Maturity.** Prophetic identity grows in stages. What begins as sensitivity grows into accuracy. What begins as impressions grows into clarity. What begins as glimpses grows into revelation.
E. **Submission.** A prepared prophet submits to God and to godly leadership. Lone rangers become dangerous voices.

The process is not punishment; it is preparation.
God does not rush prophets—He refines them.

7. THE CALL BRINGS AN AWARENESS OF DIVINE RESPONSIBILITY

A prophet's identity carries great responsibility. Revelation is not entertainment—it is assignment. Hearing God does not make a person special; it makes them responsible.

The prepared prophet understands:

• God's words must be handled with integrity

- God's timing must be respected
- God's people must be honored
- God's standards must be upheld
- God's glory must not be stolen

Prophets are entrusted with:

- instructions
- warnings
- confirmations
- encouragement
- insight
- direction
- correction

This stewardship requires:

- spiritual sobriety
- moral purity
- emotional stability
- doctrinal soundness
- relational accountability
- personal discipline

The greater the revelation, the greater the responsibility.

8. THE CALL CREATES SENSITIVITY TO THE SPIRITUAL REALM

Prophets see what others overlook. They feel what others dismiss. They sense shifts in the atmosphere. They discern spiritual influences. They understand the deeper meaning behind events. They recognize patterns, seasons, and spiritual cycles.

The prophetic identity heightens:

- spiritual perception
- discernment
- awareness of the unseen
- clarity regarding spiritual warfare
- sensitivity to the Holy Spirit
- insight into motives
- awareness of divine timing

This sensitivity is not weird or mystical—it is spiritual maturity. Prophets live with one ear to heaven and one ear to the earth, listening for the intersection of divine will and human obedience.

9. THE CALL PRODUCES BOLDNESS TO SPEAK TRUTH

A prophet's identity is forged through courage.
God does not call prophets to be popular; He calls them to be faithful.

Prophets must speak truth:

- when truth is resisted
- when truth is uncomfortable
- when truth costs relationships
- when truth confronts power
- when truth provokes change
- when truth demands repentance

This boldness is not rudeness—it is righteousness.
It does not come from personality—it comes from conviction.

The prepared prophet does not speak to be heard—they speak because God has spoken. Their boldness is anchored in intimacy with God, not the approval of people.

10. THE CALL MAKES THE PROPHET A TARGET

Spiritual calling attracts spiritual conflict.
Prophets are targets because:

- they disrupt darkness
- they expose deception
- they reveal truth
- they intercede
- they influence atmosphere
- they carry divine authority

Every prophet must expect:

- spiritual warfare
- misunderstanding
- rejection
- opposition
- criticism
- isolation

But they must never fear it.

Why?

Because God defends those He calls.
He protects those He sends.
He strengthens those He anoints.

He shields those who carry His word.

Prophets are not fragile—they are fortified by the presence of God.

11. THE CALL REQUIRES EMOTIONAL MATURITY

Prophets feel deeply.
They feel the burden of God.
They feel the pain of people.
They feel the weight of spiritual atmospheres.

But emotional depth requires emotional mastery.

A prepared prophet must learn:

- not to take rejection personally
- not to speak from woundedness
- not to confuse emotion with revelation
- not to react hastily
- not to prophesy from frustration
- not to isolate in discouragement

Prophets must develop:

- emotional resilience
- spiritual grounding
- inner stability
- patience
- self-control
- boundaries

Without emotional maturity, prophetic gifting can become distorted.

12. THE CALL SHAPES THE PROPHET'S CHARACTER

The prophetic calling does not simply shape your ministry—it shapes your character. God cares more about the vessel than the visibility.

A prepared prophet is marked by:

- integrity
- compassion
- discipline
- purity
- humility
- consistency
- wisdom
- honor

Revelation without character leads to destruction.
But revelation grounded in character leads to transformation.

Prophets must be as holy as the message they carry.

13. THE CALL DEMANDS A LIFE OF OBEDIENCE

Delayed obedience is disobedience.
Partial obedience is disobedience.
Selective obedience is disobedience.
Prophets are entrusted with divine instruction, which requires immediate, accurate obedience. The prophetic identity is tied to a prophetic response.

Obedience unlocks:

- clarity
- authority
- favor
- protection
- spiritual increase
- deeper revelation

God does not speak deeply to those who obey selectively.

14. THE CALL DEVELOPS A HEART OF COMPASSION

Popular culture portrays prophets as harsh or confrontational, but true prophetic identity is rooted in compassion. Prophets confront because they care. They warn because they love. They speak truth because they long for people to walk in God's will.

A prophet without compassion becomes cruel.
A prophet without empathy becomes abrasive.
A prophet without love becomes ineffective.

The heart of a prophet must reflect the heart of the God they represent.

15. YOU ARE NOT WHAT YOU DO — YOU ARE WHO HE CALLED YOU TO BE

Identity is not built on performance.
You are not a prophet because you prophesy.
You prophesy because you are a prophet.

Your identity precedes your assignment.
Your calling precedes your gifting.

Your purpose precedes your platform.

Prophetic identity is not found in:

- public ministry
- online influence
- church position
- spiritual gifts

Prophetic identity is rooted in:

- divine calling
- spiritual intimacy
- personal consecration
- hearing God clearly
- obeying God fully

The prepared prophet understands:
Identity is who you are.
Assignment is what you do.

Both are holy.
Both are God-given.
Both are necessary.

But identity always comes first.

CONCLUSION: THE WEIGHT IS HEAVY BECAUSE THE CALLING IS HOLY

The calling of a prophet is not light. It is weighty because it is holy. It is demanding because it is divine. It is stretching because it shapes destiny. It is confronting because it transforms character. It is costly because it carries eternal significance.

The prepared prophet embraces this calling—
not reluctantly,
not pridefully,
but reverently.

They understand that prophetic identity is not a title—it is a transformation.
It is not a role—it is a responsibility.
It is not a moment—it is a mandate.
It is not about being impressive—it is about being yielded.

This is the weight of the call.
This is the identity of the prophet.
This is the foundation of the journey ahead.

3

The Wilderness Classroom

How God Trains His Prophets in Hidden Places

INTRODUCTION: THE UNCHOSEN CLASSROOM OF DESTINY

Every prophet must learn this truth:
Before God ever uses a prophet publicly, He trains them privately

The wilderness is God's chosen academy.

It is unconventional, uncomfortable, uncelebrated, and unavoidable.

It is a place without applause, without visibility, and without recognition.

Yet it is here—away from the noise, away from distraction, away from human validation—where prophetic depth is forged.

The wilderness is not punishment; it is preparation.
It is not rejection; it is refinement.
It is not abandonment; it is appointment.

If you study the lives of every biblical prophet and major spiritual leader, you discover a consistent pattern: God leads His chosen vessels into isolation before entrusting them with impact.

Moses: 40 years in Midian
Elijah: the brook Cherith
John the Baptist: the desert
Jesus: the wilderness
Paul: Arabia
David: the shepherd fields
Samuel: the quiet of the tabernacle
Elisha: years of hidden servanthood
Joseph: prison and slavery

The wilderness is not where God forgets you.
It is where He forms you.

This chapter explores that hidden classroom—the place where prophets are shaped, purified, matured, and strengthened for their divine assignment.

1. THE WILDERNESS BEGINS WITH DIVINE DISRUPTION

No one volunteers for the wilderness.
God leads you there intentionally.
The wilderness begins with a disruption—an abrupt shift in life that dismantles your expectations and rearranges your comfort.

This disruption may come in the form of:

- a transition
- a closed door
- a betrayal
- a sudden relocation
- a painful loss
- a spiritual awakening
- a divine redirection

Why does God use disruption to begin wilderness training?

Because comfort makes you complacent, and complacency makes you deaf.

God uses disruption to get your attention.

In the wilderness, God removes:

- distractions
- idols
- unhealthy dependencies
- noise
- false expectations
- external voices

He clears the clutter so He can cultivate the prophet.

2. THE WILDERNESS IS DESIGNED TO DETOX THE SOUL

The modern world is toxic with:

- comparison

- fear
- hurry
- pride
- insecurity
- self-reliance
- emotional clutter
- spiritual numbness
- constant noise

The wilderness detoxes the soul.
It strips away everything that competes with the voice of God.

You cannot hear God clearly when:

- your heart is clogged with fear
- your mind is filled with noise
- your spirit is overwhelmed
- your identity is tied to people
- your emotions govern your decisions

The wilderness purges the prophet.
It cleanses motives.
It softens the heart.
It awakens spiritual hunger.
It separates the sacred from the superficial.

Before God fills the prophet, He empties the prophet.
The detox is painful, but it is essential.

3. THE WILDERNESS TEACHES PROPHETS TO RELY ON GOD ALONE

Every wilderness story in Scripture teaches dependence.

Moses learned dependence through isolation.
He had status in Egypt, but he needed humility in Midian.

Elijah learned dependence at Cherith.
He drank from a brook and ate from the mouths of birds—daily divine dependence.

Hagar learned dependence in her lowest moment.
God met her in the desert with provision and promise.

Israel learned dependence for 40 years.
Manna taught them God provides just enough for today.

Jesus modeled dependence in the wilderness.
Strength came not from comfort, but from communion.

Prophets must learn that:

- their source is God
- their strength is God
- their identity is in God
- their validation comes from God
- their direction comes from God

Dependence is not weakness—it is spiritual maturity.
The prepared prophet learns:
If God is all you have, God is all you need.

4. THE WILDERNESS TEACHES STILLNESS AND SILENCE

Modern believers are addicted to noise.

Prophets cannot be.

One of the most uncomfortable lessons in the wilderness is silence.

Silence reveals:

- what you fear
- what you avoid
- what you suppress
- what you depend on
- what you idolize
- what you believe

Silence exposes the soul.

But in silence, God teaches the prophet to:

- become still
- listen deeply
- wait patiently
- perceive spiritually
- trust fully

Stillness is not inactivity—it is attentiveness.
It is the discipline of quieting the inner life so the voice of God becomes unmistakable.

Prophets cannot operate from noise.
They must learn the language of silence—the place where revelation is born.

5. THE WILDERNESS BREAKS THE POWER OF PEOPLE-PLEASING

Prophets cannot be controlled by people's opinions.
They cannot fear rejection or crave applause.
They cannot be governed by expectations or manipulated by emotions.

In the wilderness, God removes the illusion of human security.
He teaches the prophet to find approval in Him alone.

Here, the prophet learns:

- people didn't call you
- people can't anoint you
- people didn't choose you
- people can't define you
- people won't sustain you
- people can't cancel what God ordained

Until a prophet is free from people, they can never speak freely to people.

The wilderness breaks the grip of human approval.

6. THE WILDERNESS TEACHES OBEDIENCE IN HIDDENNESS

Public obedience earns applause.
Private obedience earns authority.

Most of a prophet's obedience will never be seen by people.
It will be seen only by God.

Prophets are formed in hidden obedience:

- praying when no one knows
- studying when no one is watching
- fasting when no one sees
- serving without recognition
- repenting without exposure
- obeying without reward

Hidden obedience shapes prophetic authority.

God will not trust a prophet publicly until they prove themselves obedient privately.

The wilderness is where He tests that obedience.

7. THE WILDERNESS SHARPENS DISCERNMENT

Discernment is not suspicion.
It is spiritual sensitivity.

Prophets must discern:

- God's voice
- God's will
- spiritual atmospheres
- demonic influences
- human motives
- hidden dangers
- divine timing
- doors God opens
- doors God closes

Discernment cannot be taught in classrooms.

It is born in the wilderness through:

- solitude
- prayer
- fasting
- quietness
- trial
- testing
- reflection

The wilderness becomes a prophetic training ground where the fog of confusion lifts and spiritual clarity develops.

8. THE WILDERNESS CONFRONTS THE PROPHET'S CHARACTER

Gifts attract people.
Character attracts God.

In the wilderness, God confronts:

- pride
- jealousy
- insecurity
- impatience
- comparison
- anger
- stubbornness
- bitterness
- self-promotion

The wilderness reveals the prophet to themselves.

Here, God says:
"You cannot go forward with that in you."

The wilderness purifies motives.
It uproots toxic tendencies.
It dismantles ego.
It heals inner wounds.
It strengthens weak places.
It stabilizes emotional immaturity.

A prophet cannot carry the weight of divine responsibility without character formation.

The wilderness is the refining fire.

9. THE WILDERNESS TEACHES THE VOICE OF GOD THROUGH CONTRAST

One of the most profound truths of the wilderness is this:

You learn God's voice faster in isolation than in activity.

Why?

Because in the wilderness, the voices of:

- culture
- ministry
- expectations
- obligations
- distractions

- routines

...are silenced.

This contrast makes the voice of God clearer, stronger, and purer.

Prophets learn the difference between:

- God's voice vs. their thoughts
- God's leading vs. their emotions
- God's timing vs. their impulse
- God's direction vs. people's demands

The wilderness teaches prophetic hearing without interference.

10. THE WILDERNESS BREAKS THE PROPHET'S DEPENDENCE ON COMFORT

Comfort is the greatest enemy of calling.

Prophets cannot develop in comfort.
Comfort kills urgency.
Comfort dulls sensitivity.
Comfort creates spiritual apathy.

The wilderness disrupts comfort so the prophet learns:

- endurance
- perseverance
- strength
- focus
- inner resilience

Wilderness seasons require:

- spiritual toughness
- mental fortitude
- emotional stability
- unwavering faith

Prophets cannot be fragile.
They must be forged.

The wilderness hardens the spirit in the best way—making the prophet unshakeable.

11. THE WILDERNESS PRODUCES A FOUNDATION OF INTIMACY

The true goal of the wilderness is intimacy with God.

Prophets are not shaped by gifting—they are shaped by intimacy.

In the wilderness, the prophet learns:

- how to hear God
- how to feel God
- how to respond to God
- how to trust God
- how to walk with God

Intimacy becomes the prophet's anchor.
It is what sustains them through:

- warfare
- rejection
- assignment
- responsibility
- spiritual pressure

A prophet without intimacy is dangerous.
A prophet with intimacy is unstoppable.

12. THE WILDERNESS EXPOSES HIDDEN IDOLS

Prophets must confront the idols they did not know they had.

Idols of:

- control
- reputation
- security
- relationships
- success
- ministry
- personal dreams
- identity
- comfort

The wilderness exposes these idols so the prophet can surrender them.

Until idols fall, revelation is limited.
Until idols break, destiny cannot unfold.

The wilderness sets the prophet free.

13. THE WILDERNESS IS THE PLACE OF DIVINE REVELATION

While the wilderness is a place of stripping, it is also a place of revelation.

Prophets receive some of their greatest encounters in isolation.

Moses received the burning bush.
Elijah heard the still small voice.
John the Baptist heard divine instruction.
Jesus received strength and clarity.
John received the book of Revelation.

The wilderness gives:

- visions
- dreams
- direction
- instruction
- strategies
- correction
- encounters
- mpartation

Isolation becomes incubation.
Hiddenness becomes holiness.
Silence becomes strength.

Prophets come out of the wilderness with revelation that cannot be learned anywhere else.

14. THE WILDERNESS IS TEMPORARY BUT TRANSFORMATIONAL

No wilderness season lasts forever.
It is a season, not a life sentence.
It is a chapter, not the whole book.

But once a prophet leaves the wilderness, they are:

- stronger
- wiser
- clearer
- deeper
- more mature
- more discerning
- more surrendered
- more obedient
- more anointed

The wilderness changes everything.

Prophets emerge transformed—ready for the weight of divine assignment.

15. *The Prophet's Graduation From the Wilderness*

Every wilderness has a graduation moment.
It is when God says:

- "Now."
- "Go."
- "Speak."
- "Step forward."

- "Your season of hiding is over."

Moses emerged with a staff and a mission.
David emerged with anointing and authority.
Joseph emerged with wisdom and influence.
Jesus emerged with power and purpose.

The wilderness is not where destiny dies.
It is where destiny develops.

The prepared prophet graduates with:

- confidence
- authority
- identity
- clarity
- maturity
- divine backing
- prophetic precision

What emerges from the wilderness is not the same person who entered it.

CONCLUSION: THE WILDERNESS IS GOD'S SEAL OF AUTHENTICITY

If you have been in a wilderness season, it is not a sign of disqualification—
it is a sign of preparation.

The wilderness proves:

- God is with you

- God is shaping you
- God is strengthening you
- God is preparing you
- God is calling you
- God is trusting you

The wilderness is not easy, but it is essential.
It is not glamorous, but it is glorious.
It is not comfortable, but it is transformative.

This is the classroom of the prepared prophet.
This is where God molds His messengers.
This is where prophetic identity is deepened and divine purpose revealed.

You are not being buried—you are being planted.
You are not being punished—you are being prepared.
You are not being forgotten—you are being formed.

The wilderness is God's workshop, and you are His masterpiece.

4

Hearing Beyond the Noise

Developing Discernment in a Distracted World

INTRODUCTION: A LOUD WORLD AND A WHISPERING GOD

We live in the loudest generation in human history.
Everyone has a voice.
Everyone has a platform.
Everyone has an opinion.
Everyone has an angle, a narrative, an agenda, or a message.

Noise comes from every direction—
television, social media, notifications, conversations, responsibilities, politics, culture, expectations, and even internal fears and doubts.

This is not accidental.
The enemy does not need to silence a believer to defeat them.

He only needs to distract them.

A distracted Christian is as ineffective as a disobedient one.
A distracted prophet is as dangerous as a deceived one.

The prophetic life requires discernment, and discernment requires quietness.

Not the quietness of inactivity—but the quietness of spirit that allows a prophet to hear beyond the world's noise, beyond their own thoughts, beyond their emotions, and beyond demonic deception.

This chapter is the training ground for prophets learning to tune their ears to heaven in a culture drowning in noise.

1. DISCERNMENT BEGINS WITH SPIRITUAL LISTENING

Discernment is not suspicion, intuition, or common sense.

Discernment is the spiritual ability to perceive the true source, intent, and nature of a thing.

Discernment is:

- sensing the unseen
- perceiving motives
- recognizing deception
- identifying the voice of God
- distinguishing between voices
- detecting spiritual atmospheres
- receiving divine insight instantly
- separating truth from almost-truth

Discernment begins with spiritual listening—not listening with your natural ears, but with the ears of your spirit.

Prophets must "hear behind the hearing."

They listen to:

- what is said
- what is not said
- what is implied
- what is spiritual
- what is hidden
- what is influencing
- what is driving decisions
- what is stirring atmospheres

Spiritual listening is deeper than hearing words.
It is perceiving realities.

2. THE THREE VOICES EVERY PROPHET MUST DISTINGUISH

Every prophet must learn to separate three primary voices:

A. The Voice of God

Pure. Holy. Peaceful. Convicting. Clear. Authoritative.
The voice of God aligns with Scripture, produces life, and leads to obedience.

B. The Voice of the Flesh

Emotional. Impulsive. Opinionated. Fearful. Self-centered.
The flesh sounds urgent, worried, frustrated, or self-protective.

C. The Voice of the Enemy

Subtle. Manipulative. Condemning. Confusing. Deceptive.
The enemy mixes truth with lies, creating spiritual distraction.

Prophets cannot mature until they can instantly differentiate between these three voices.

This is learned in:

- silence
- solitude
- Scripture
- prayer
- testing
- waiting
- practice

Discernment is not automatic—
it is developed.

3. NOISE IS THE ENEMY OF DISCERNMENT

Noise is not just audible sound.
Noise is anything that competes with the voice of God.

This includes:

- internal noise (fear, anxiety, insecurity)
- emotional noise (offense, anger, excitement)
- mental noise (overthinking, planning, problem-solving)
- spiritual noise (demonic interference)

- social noise (media, friends, expectations)
- cultural noise (trends, political narratives, influences)

Noise clouds spiritual perception.
Noise distorts prophetic accuracy.
Noise dulls sensitivity to Holy Spirit whispers.

Prophets must be ruthless in reducing noise.

The quieter the soul,
the clearer the Spirit.

4. DISCERNMENT REQUIRES THE DISCIPLINE OF STILLNESS

Stillness is a lost art in modern Christianity.
Yet it is essential for prophetic clarity.

Stillness means:

- quieting the heart
- calming the mind
- listening intentionally
- waiting without rushing
- being fully present with God
- resisting the urge to fill silence with activity

Stillness is where prophets learn:

- God's tone
- God's rhythm
- God's timing
- God's patterns

- God's nature
- God's impressions
- God's whisper

You cannot sense God's whisper while rushing.
You cannot discern His guidance while stressed.
You cannot detect His leading while distracted.

Stillness is strength.
Stillness is training.
Stillness is prophetic survival.

5. DISCERNMENT DEEPENS IN THE SCRIPTURES

Discernment is impossible without Scripture.
The Bible is the standard that judges all revelation.

God's voice will never:

- contradict Scripture
- bypass Scripture
- diminish Scripture
- distort Scripture
- replace Scripture

The more Word a prophet has in their spirit,
the more accurately they will discern the voice of God.

Scripture trains the prophet to:

- recognize God's character
- understand spiritual principles
- discern false doctrine

- perceive divine patterns
- identify deception
- test prophetic impressions

The prepared prophet is not just spiritually sensitive—they are biblically grounded.

Discernment without Scripture is deception.
Scripture without discernment is limitation.
But Scripture with discernment is revelation.

6. DISCERNMENT REQUIRES INNER PURITY

The unpurified heart distorts discernment.

A prophet cannot discern clearly when clouded by:

- offense
- bitterness
- jealousy
- pride
- insecurity
- unforgiveness
- emotional wounds
- hidden sin

Impure motives distort spiritual perception.
The heart becomes biased, reactive, or defensive.

Purity produces clarity.
Purity sharpens sensitivity.
Purity prepares the prophet.

The prepared prophet prays:

"Lord, purify my heart so I can perceive Your voice."

Discernment is as much a heart issue as a spiritual skill.

7. DISCERNMENT IS STRENGTHENED THROUGH SPIRITUAL PRACTICES

Prophets develop discernment through spiritual disciplines:

A. **Prayer.** Deep prayer heightens spiritual awareness.
B. **Fasting.** Fasting breaks flesh, sharpens spirit, and increases clarity.
C. **Worship.** Prophetic environments increase sensitivity.
D. **Solitude.** Isolation removes interference.
E. **Journaling.** Writing impressions clarifies patterns.
F. **Listening Prayer.** Stillness trains the inner ear.
G. **Intercession.** Intercession opens prophetic perception.
H. **Repetition.** The more you listen, the better you hear.

Discernment grows like a muscle—
through consistent use.

8. DISCERNMENT PROTECTS THE PROPHET FROM DECEPTION

Deception is the greatest threat to prophetic ministry.
The enemy uses:

- counterfeit voices
- emotional manipulation
- spiritual intimidation

- imitation revelations
- false confirmations
- distorted impressions

A prophet without discernment will:

- misinterpret God
- misread people
- mistake emotion for revelation
- believe lies
- follow flattery
- be swayed by pressure
- fall into error
- damage people

Discernment is the prophet's shield.
Without it, prophetic gifting becomes dangerous.

The prepared prophet must master discernment before mastering revelation.

9. DISCERNMENT EXPOSES MOTIVES

Prophets do more than hear words—
they perceive motives.

Discernment allows prophets to see:

- the heart behind actions
- intentions behind words

- hidden agendas
- unspoken needs
- spiritual vulnerabilities
- emotional wounds
- patterns of behavior
- sources of influence

Prophets do not judge people—
they discern influences.

Discernment reveals:

- brokenness
- manipulation
- immaturity
- sincerity
- deception
- divine appointments
- demonic assignments

Prophetic ministry requires the ability to separate the person from the spirit influencing them.

This clarity protects both the prophet and the people they minister to.

10. DISCERNMENT HELPS THE PROPHET RECOGNIZE DIVINE TIMING

Discernment is not only about hearing God—
it is about understanding when God is speaking.

Timing is everything in the prophetic.

A word delivered at the wrong time can:

- cause confusion
- create premature action
- produce unnecessary warfare
- mislead the listener
- hinder the assignment

Discernment reveals:

- when to speak
- when to wait
- when to pray
- when to act
- when to be silent
- when to confront
- when to encourage
- when to rest

The prepared prophet learns that timing is prophetic wisdom.

Without discernment of timing, even accurate words can have harmful results.

11. DISCERNMENT DEVELOPS THROUGH TESTING WHAT YOU HEAR

God never rebukes prophets for testing revelation.
Testing is part of prophetic maturity.

Prophets must test:

- impressions
- dreams
- visions
- burdens
- warnings
- spiritual senses
- sudden insights
- inner prompts

Testing includes evaluating:

A. **Alignment with Scripture.** If it contradicts Scripture, it is not God.
B. **Agreement with God's character.** God does not speak in ways inconsistent with His nature.
C. **Confirmation by the Holy Spirit.** Peace accompanies truth. Trouble accompanies deception.
D. **Repetition.** True revelation often repeats itself.
E. **Wisdom.** God's voice is wise, not reckless.
F. **Godly counsel.** Mature leaders confirm direction.
G. **Outcome.** God's words bear fruit of righteousness.

Testing refines discernment and prevents error.

12. Discernment Reveals Spiritual Atmospheres

Prophets can sense what is happening spiritually in a room, a region, a relationship, or a situation.

Discernment reveals:

- demonic oppression
- spiritual resistance

- divine favor
- angelic activity
- prophetic stirring
- grief of the Spirit
- spiritual hunger
- divine opportunities
- dangerous influences

Atmospheres preach.
Environments speak.
Spiritual climates shift.

Prophets must learn to discern not just words, but atmospheres.

Prophets walk into a room and immediately sense:

"This is heavy,"
"This is holy,"
"This is resistant,"
"This is peaceful,"
"This is confused,"
"This is strategic."

Atmospheric discernment is essential to effective prophetic ministry.

13. DISCERNMENT HELPS PROPHETS AVOID EMOTIONAL PROPHECY

Emotion is powerful.
Emotion is persuasive.
Emotion is dangerous when mistaken for revelation.

A prophet must be careful not to prophesy from:

- excitement
- fear
- sadness
- anger
- disappointment
- stress
- adrenaline
- personal preference

Emotional prophecy may feel spiritual,
but it is spiritually harmful.

Discernment teaches the prophet to:

- separate emotion from revelation
- identify when their feelings are speaking
- recognize when their flesh is influencing the word
- wait until emotions settle before speaking
- avoid impulsive prophetic declarations

Pure discernment requires emotional stability.

14. DISCERNMENT HELPS PROPHETS GUIDE OTHERS SAFELY

Prophets are guides—spiritual navigators helping people follow God's will.

Without discernment, a prophet can:

- mislead

- misinterpret
- misjudge
- misdirect
- mishandle souls
- misrepresent God

But with discernment, prophets can:

- protect
- counsel
- warn
- direct
- affirm
- build
- restore
- guide

Discernment makes prophetic ministry safe.

The prepared prophet is not only accurate—
they are wise.

15. DISCERNMENT REQUIRES SPIRITUAL MATURITY

Discernment grows as the prophet grows.

Immature prophets:

- assume impressions are always God
- react emotionally
- misread situations
- trust every spiritual feeling

- prophesy prematurely
- confuse suspicion with revelation
- lack spiritual discipline

Mature prophets:

- test what they hear
- wait on God
- stay scripturally grounded
- discern motives
- recognize manipulation
- avoid emotional entanglement
- follow peace
- remain accountable

Discernment is the fruit of spiritual maturity, not the result of spiritual excitement.

16. DISCERNMENT HELPS PROPHETS NAVIGATE SPIRITUAL WARFARE

Prophets are targets.
Discernment reveals:

- when warfare is rising
- where it is coming from
- what the enemy is using
- how to respond
- when to pray
- when to speak
- when to be silent
- when to resist
- when to retreat

- when to stand still

Discernment allows prophets to stay one step ahead of the enemy.

Without discernment, prophets walk into traps.
With discernment, prophets dismantle them.

17. DISCERNMENT GROWS THROUGH REPETITION AND REVELATION

The more a prophet listens, the better they hear.
The more they hear, the more they recognize.
The more they recognize, the more they trust.

Discernment is built through:

- repeated exposure to God's voice
- repeated testing of impressions
- repeated obedience
- repeated reflection
- repeated encounters
- repeated spiritual victories

Discernment is a lifelong journey.
Prophets do not graduate from it—
they grow deeper in it.

18. DISCERNMENT IS THE PROPHET'S SURVIVAL SKILL

Discernment keeps the prophet:

- accurate
- pure
- safe
- stable
- effective
- humble
- obedient
- grounded
- empowered

Without discernment, prophets fall.
With discernment, prophets flourish.

Discernment separates the gifted from the prepared.
It separates the excited from the established.
It separates the emotional from the spiritual.
It separates the impulsive from the obedient.

Discernment is the survival skill that sustains prophetic calling.

19. THE DISCERNMENT PRAYER OF THE PREPARED PROPHET

A prophet's greatest weapon is a discerning heart.

Pray this:

"Lord, sharpen my spirit.
Quiet my soul.
Strengthen my discernment.
Teach me to hear You above all voices.
Purify my motives.
Sanctify my imagination.

Illuminate my understanding.
Guard me from deception.
Train my ears to recognize Your whisper.
Make me a prophet who hears beyond the noise."

This is the prayer of a prepared prophet.

CONCLUSION: DISCERNMENT IS THE PROPHET'S EAR TO HEAVEN

Discernment is not optional for a prophet—
it is essential.

You cannot carry God's message without hearing His voice.
You cannot speak truth without separating it from noise.
You cannot guide others if you cannot guide yourself.
You cannot stand in purity without discerning deception.
You cannot serve God fully without hearing Him clearly.

Discernment is the compass of the prepared prophet.
It is the inner ear tuned to heaven's frequency.
It is the spiritual clarity that guides every decision, every word, every assignment.

In a distracted world, the prophet must become a sanctuary of stillness.
In a loud generation, the prophet must be a listener of God.
In a confused culture, the prophet must hear beyond the noise.

This is the way of the prepared prophet.
This is your calling—
to hear heaven clearly
and reveal it faithfully.

5

Prophetic Intimacy

Cultivating a Friendship With God

INTRODUCTION: THE CALLING TO WALK WITH GOD, NOT WORK FOR HIM

Every prophet must eventually recognize that prophetic power does not come from spiritual activity, but from relational proximity. It is possible to minister for God while living far from Him. It is possible to prophesy accurately while praying inconsistently. It is even possible to carry gifts while lacking intimacy. Many believers pursue prophetic ability, but very few pursue prophetic closeness. Yet the greatest prophetic secret in the Bible is simple: God reveals His secrets to His friends.

Prophetic intimacy is not about earning revelation through effort; it is about receiving revelation through relationship. God speaks most clearly to those who walk with Him most closely. This chapter explores the heart of prophetic maturity—cultivating a deep, personal, consistent, and transformative friendship with God that prepares the prophet to hear Him with clarity and reflect Him with purity.

1. INTIMACY IS THE TRUE FOUNDATION OF PROPHETIC MINISTRY

Prophetic ministry is not first about speaking for God; it is about being with God. Many desire the prophetic mantle, the prophetic accuracy, and the prophetic authority, but few commit to the prophetic closeness required to sustain it. Intimacy with God is not an optional discipline; it is the prophet's very lifeline.

Prophetic intimacy is not measured by how much you know, but by how deeply you are known by God. It is not defined by the number of visions, dreams, or revelations you receive, but by the depth of your daily communion with the Spirit.

When intimacy is the foundation, revelation becomes natural, obedience becomes joyful, and holiness becomes a desire rather than a duty. Without intimacy, the prophetic quickly becomes mechanical, burdensome, and even dangerous, because the prophet begins to give words that come from their gift instead of their God.

True prophetic authority flows from proximity, not performance.

2. GOD INVITES PROPHETS INTO FRIENDSHIP, NOT JUST SERVICE

Throughout Scripture, we see that God treated His prophets not merely as servants, but as friends. He walked with Enoch. He called Abraham His friend. He spoke with Moses "face to face," as one speaks with a companion. He opened His heart to Jeremiah, allowing him to feel divine grief. He revealed His mysteries to Daniel in quiet places of prayer. Jesus told His disciples that servants do not know their master's private intentions, but friends do—and He considered them friends.

This is not poetic language. It is divine invitation.

The prophetic life is not built on duty; it is sustained by relationship. The prophet is not merely an employee of Heaven tasked with delivering messages; the prophet is a confidant of God who receives revelation because of intimacy.

Friendship with God means:

- You desire Him even when you desire nothing else.
- You pursue Him apart from platform or responsibility.
- You listen to Him even when He says nothing about ministry.
- You spend time with Him simply because He is worthy of your presence.

The prepared prophet must understand that intimacy is not an accessory—it is the essence of prophetic life.

3. INTIMACY DEVELOPS THROUGH CONSISTENT, HONEST PRAYER

Prophetic intimacy is cultivated in the quiet, unhurried, honest moments of prayer where the soul reveals itself and the Spirit responds. Prayer is not a ritual; it is relationship. It is not a speech; it is conversation. It is not a religious obligation; it is a relational invitation.

Many people pray to check a devotional box, but prophets pray to commune with the heart of God. Their prayers are not merely requests but reflections. They speak, but they also listen. They express, but they also receive. They pour out their hearts, but they also allow God to pour into them. The prophet understands that prayer is not a task to complete—it is a place of connection.

This kind of prayer is honest. It reveals doubts, confesses failures, expresses fears, and embraces vulnerability. Prophetic intimacy does not require perfection; it requires authenticity. God does not draw near to the perfect. He draws near to the sincere.

Prophets who prioritize honest prayer develop spiritual sensitivity. They become familiar with the tone of God's voice, the rhythm of His presence, and the way His Spirit whispers. Their hearts become a sanctuary where revelation is natural and communion is continual.

4. INTIMACY GROWS THROUGH SCRIPTURE THAT SHAPES THE SOUL

Prophets must become students of Scripture—not for information, but for transformation. The Bible is not merely a reference manual; it is the expression of God's heart, nature, and character. The prophet who wishes to know the voice of God must first know the Word of God.

Scripture anchors revelation. It balances emotion. It purifies motives. It corrects error. It trains the inner ear to recognize God's tone. Through Scripture, prophets learn how God speaks, how He moves, what He values, and how He responds to His people.

Reading the Bible devotionally, not merely academically, is essential for prophetic intimacy. The goal is not to find material for sermon notes or prophetic messages, but to draw near to the One who authored the text. When the prophet reads Scripture with hunger and humility, God speaks through passages that penetrate the heart, awaken conviction, and strengthen identity.

Intimacy grows every time the prophet opens the Bible and asks, "Lord, show me who You are."

5. INTIMACY REQUIRES TIME, NOT JUST EMOTION

Many believers pursue emotional encounters with God, but intimacy requires consistent time. A prophet cannot build a deep spiritual life through occasional inspiration. Consistency creates depth. Patterns produce power. Habits form holiness.

The prophet learns to set aside intentional, protected time for God—not the leftovers of a busy day, but the firstfruits of their attention. This time may include reading, worship, prayer, silence, reflection, listening, or simply sitting in the presence of God without rushing.

God does not measure intimacy by passion but by priority. Anyone can feel spiritually excited during a worship song, but the prophet who chooses consistent communion demonstrates true devotion. Emotional connection may come and go, but commitment sustains relationship.

Intimacy is not built in one dramatic encounter; it is built in thousands of small moments of intentional closeness.

6. INTIMACY DEEPENS WHEN THE PROPHET LEARNS TO LISTEN, NOT JUST SPEAK

Most people approach prayer as though they are the only ones speaking. But prophets grow in intimacy when they learn the beauty of listening prayer. Listening prayer requires patience, stillness, and a quieted soul. It means waiting on God without impatience, surrendering control over the moment, and giving space for the Spirit to speak.

Listening prayer teaches prophets:

- how to recognize impressions
- how to discern divine prompting
- how to perceive revelation that comes softly

- how to identify shifts in spiritual atmosphere
- how to distinguish God's voice from internal noise

Listening is not passive; it is profoundly active. It demands attention, humility, and presence. When the prophet listens, God does not always speak in words. Sometimes He speaks through peace, conviction, clarity, awareness, or a sudden sense of direction.

Listening builds intimacy because it demonstrates desire, reverence, and expectation.

7. INTIMACY REQUIRES YIELDING, NOT CONTROLLING

Prophetic people often feel deeply, sense strongly, and perceive quickly. This intensity can lead to a desire to control spiritual outcomes. But intimacy requires surrender. It means trusting God even when He does not reveal His full plan. It means embracing His timing, His methods, and His pace.

Surrender deepens intimacy because it removes barriers. God reveals more to the prophet who is willing to obey without condition. The more the prophet yields, the more God shares. Revelation increases with surrender. Obedience unlocks intimacy. Trust draws God near.

Intimacy is not about understanding everything—it is about trusting Him in everything.

8. INTIMACY WITH GOD HEALS THE WOUNDS OF THE PROPHET

Prophets feel deeply. They carry burdens, sense spiritual oppression, experience rejection, and often face loneliness. Without intimacy with God, these wounds can produce bitterness, insecurity, or emotional instability.

But in intimacy, God heals. He restores confidence. He strengthens the soul. He calms anxiety. He lifts burdens. He comforts pain. He restores identity.

Prophets can be hyper-sensitive to spiritual environments but often unaware of their own emotional needs. Intimate time with God becomes a place of healing, recalibration, and rest. It protects the prophet from burnout and keeps their heart pure.

The wounded prophet becomes whole in the presence of the Healer.

9. INTIMACY PRODUCES HOLINESS THAT CANNOT BE COUNTERFEITED

Prophetic accuracy without holiness is dangerous. Intimacy purifies the prophet's heart, motives, desires, and decisions. It strengthens character and produces humility. Only intimacy can create sustainable holiness, because holiness is not merely moral behavior—it is relational closeness.

When the prophet draws near to God, sins lose their attraction. Temptation loses its grip. Compromise becomes unthinkable. Intimacy transforms holiness from obligation to desire.

Holiness produced by intimacy is authentic, gentle, consistent, and deeply rooted in love. It becomes the environment where revelation flows freely.

10. INTIMACY STRENGTHENS THE PROPHET IN TIMES OF SILENCE

There will be seasons when God feels silent. These seasons are not punishment—they are invitations. God often uses silence to test maturity, deepen trust, and purify motives. In silence, prophets discover whether they seek God for His voice or for His presence.

Intimacy teaches prophets that God's silence does not mean His absence. He is just as present in the quiet as He is in moments of revelation. Prophets who have cultivated intimacy do not panic when they cannot immediately hear God; instead, they rest in the relationship they have built over time.

Intimacy creates stability in silence. It anchors the prophet when revelation temporarily pauses.

11. INTIMACY SUSTAINS PROPHETS UNDER WEIGHTY ASSIGNMENTS

Prophetic assignments often demand courage, resilience, and endurance. Some messages are comforting, but others confront darkness, expose deception, or require great emotional strength.

Without intimacy, the weight of the prophetic call becomes too heavy. But intimate friendship with God gives prophets courage to speak truth, strength to withstand resistance, and peace to deliver difficult messages.

Intimacy sustains what assignment demands.

12. INTIMACY PRODUCES THE PROPHET'S HIDDEN STRENGTH

Every public word a prophet speaks is rooted in private devotion. Their authority is not developed on platforms but in prayer closets. Their clarity comes from intimacy. Their confidence comes from communion. Their purity comes from proximity to God's presence.

The greatest prophetic strength is always hidden. The most anointed prophets are the most prayerful prophets. Their relationship with God is their reservoir of power.

The prepared prophet understands that every miracle, every revelation, every vision, and every message is born in the unseen places of intimacy.

CONCLUSION: INTIMACY IS THE PROPHET'S HOME, NOT THEIR VISIT

Prophetic intimacy is not a temporary season; it is a permanent lifestyle. It is the place where the prophet belongs. It is where the prophetic call is nourished, where the inward life is refined, and where the voice of God becomes unmistakably clear.

Without intimacy, prophets become hollow. With intimacy, they become unshakeable.

This is the heart of the prepared prophet:
a life anchored in deep friendship with God,
a spirit sensitive to His whispers,
a heart aligned with His desires,
and a soul that delights in His nearness.

The prophet who walks in intimacy never walks alone, never speaks empty words, and never loses their way. They live in the presence of the One who called them, and from that place, they carry His voice to the world.

6

⚜

The Anatomy of a Prophetic Word

INTRODUCTION: A WORD FROM GOD IS MORE THAN A MESSAGE

When a prophet speaks, it should not merely be the release of information; it should be the expression of divine intention. A prophetic word is not just a sentence, a phrase, or a prediction—it is a sacred deposit from the heart of God delivered into the heart of humanity. It carries weight, purpose, timing, emotion, accuracy, and spiritual consequence.

Many people believe that prophecy is simply "hearing God and repeating what He said," but the reality is far more nuanced. Prophetic words have structure. They have layers. They have spiritual anatomy. They contain a mixture of revelation, interpretation, timing, emotional tone, and delivery style, all of which must be handled responsibly. Prophets grow in maturity when they understand how to recognize, receive, process, interpret, and deliver a prophetic word with precision and purity.

This chapter explores the anatomy of a prophetic word so that every prepared prophet can steward revelation with excellence and faithfulness.

1. A PROPHETIC WORD BEGINS AS REVELATION FROM GOD

Every prophetic message originates with revelation—a moment when the Holy Spirit communicates something to the spirit of the prophet. Revelation is not always dramatic; sometimes it arrives gently, unexpectedly, or quietly. Revelation can come through a sudden idea, an inner impression, a dream, a vision, a Scripture that becomes alive in a unique way, or a deep spiritual knowing that bypasses human logic.

Revelation is not forced. It is not the result of imagination or emotional desire. It is the Spirit initiating communication. Prophets must learn to recognize when God is speaking, rather than mistaking internal noise or personal thoughts for divine instruction.

Revelation often carries a spiritual tone—peace, conviction, clarity, weight, urgency, or holiness. The more the prophet grows in intimacy, the easier it becomes to detect the difference between revelation and imagination. A prophetic word begins with an encounter before it becomes a message.

2. REVELATION MUST BE FOLLOWED BY INTERPRETATION

Many prophets have heard accurately but spoken prematurely because they never paused to interpret what God revealed. Revelation is perfect because it comes from God. Interpretation, however, is imperfect because it flows through human understanding.

A prophet may receive:

- an image
- a symbolic dream
- a simple phrase
- a Scripture
- a spiritual impression
- an internal awareness
- a vision containing layers

...but the meaning is not always immediately clear.

Interpretation requires:

- humility
- patience
- biblical grounding
- discernment
- prayer
- wisdom
- stillness

The prepared prophet understands that God often reveals truth in symbolic, metaphorical, or layered ways, inviting the prophet into conversation and reflection. Interpretation is where revelation is shaped into clarity.

3. TIMING IS AN ESSENTIAL PART OF THE PROPHETIC WORD

A prophetic word is not complete until timing has been discerned. Many prophetic mistakes are not errors of revelation but errors of timing. A true word spoken at the wrong time can produce confusion, fear, misdirection, or premature action.

Some words are meant for:

- now
- the near future
- a distant season
- private reflection
- intercession
- a specific moment
- a particular transition
- preparation rather than action

Prophets must ask, "When does God intend for this word to be released or fulfilled?"

Timing often becomes clear through:

- spiritual peace
- repeated confirmation
- situational alignment
- inward release
- external circumstances aligning with the word

When the prophet waits on God's timing, the word carries life. When spoken prematurely, it carries unnecessary weight.

4. A PROPHETIC WORD CARRIES A BURDEN OR EMOTION FROM GOD

Prophetic words are not emotionless messages; they carry the spiritual tone of God's heart. Some words carry compassion that heals. Others carry urgency that warns. Some carry joy that strengthens. Others carry conviction meant to awaken repentance. The emotion of a prophetic word communicates the heart of the Father behind the message.

Prophetic emotion should not be confused with human emotion. The two are very different. Divine emotion carries:

- purity
- clarity
- love
- righteous intensity
- spiritual weight

Human emotion carries inconsistency, personal reaction, and bias. To steward a prophetic word well, the prophet must distinguish between the emotion God is communicating and the emotion they personally feel.

When the prophet carries God's heart accurately, the word becomes a conduit of divine compassion, not human passion.

5. THE PROPHETIC WORD MUST BE FILTERED THROUGH SCRIPTURE

Revelation is never complete until it is filtered through the lens of Scripture. Prophets must ask:

"Does this align with the heart of God revealed in His Word?"
"Does this contradict any biblical principle or command?"
"Is this consistent with the nature, character, and ways of God?"
"Does this encourage righteousness, repentance, or edification?"

Every prophetic message must submit to the authority of Scripture. If a word contradicts Scripture, the interpretation is wrong, not the Bible. Scripture provides safety, clarity, and theological grounding.

It ensures the word aligns with the eternal truth of God rather than cultural influence, emotional desire, or personal bias.

The most mature prophets are not those with the greatest revelations, but those with the deepest commitment to biblical integrity.

6. THE MOTIVE BEHIND A PROPHETIC WORD MUST BE PURE

Prophetic ministry becomes dangerous when motives are impure. A prophetic word must never be spoken to:

- impress people
- earn influence
- manipulate decisions
- appear spiritual
- prove one's calling
- compete with others
- satisfy emotional desires
- resolve personal anxieties

A prophetic word is holy. It is not a tool for personal elevation. The prophet must examine their heart before delivering a word. If the motive is anything other than obedience to God and love for the person receiving the message, the word must wait.

Pure motives protect both the prophet and the receiver. Pure motives preserve the credibility of the prophetic. Pure motives honor the God who entrusted the revelation.

7. DELIVERY IS PART OF THE PROPHETIC ANATOMY

A prophetic word may be accurate in content, correct in interpretation, and appropriate in timing, but if it is delivered poorly, it can create unnecessary confusion or harm. Delivery is the art of prophetic communication.

Delivery involves:

- tone
- posture
- clarity
- compassion
- maturity
- wisdom
- respect
- grace
- humility

A prophetic word must be delivered in a spirit that reflects the gentleness and strength of God. It should not be spoken in anger, pride, or urgency unless God has clearly conveyed those emotions. It should not be shouted simply for dramatic effect or whispered simply to appear mysterious.

The prophet must deliver the word with emotional intelligence, spiritual sensitivity, and relational awareness. A well-delivered word builds faith. A poorly delivered word creates confusion.

8. EVERY PROPHETIC WORD HAS A PURPOSE

Prophecy is never random. Every word has purpose. Prophets must understand the assignment attached to the revelation. Prophetic words carry divine intentions.

Some prophetic words are given to:

1. Encourage. God strengthens weary hearts.

2. Correct. God redirects wrong paths.

3. Warn. God protects people from danger.

4. Prepare. God reveals what is coming.

5. Confirm. God affirms what has already been sensed.

6. Reveal identity. God speaks to who a person really is.

7. Provide instruction. God guides decisions and direction.

8. Release breakthrough. God shifts spiritual atmospheres and lifts burdens.

Understanding the purpose helps the prophet deliver the word with the proper tone and clarity.

9. PROPHETIC WORDS MUST BE STEWARDED PRIVATELY BEFORE BEING RELEASED PUBLICLY

Many revelations are not meant to be spoken immediately. Some are invitations to prayer. Others are warnings meant for intercession. Some are insights that need divine timing. Others are promises meant to strengthen the prophet's faith.

The prepared prophet understands that not every word is for public release.

A prophetic word must be:

- written down
- prayed through
- tested
- confirmed
- weighed
- refined
- clarified

Private stewardship leads to public accuracy. Prophets who speak too quickly often misinterpret what they receive. Prophets who wait on God speak with clarity and authority.

10. PROPHETIC WORDS MUST BE DELIVERED WITH ACCOUNTABILITY

Prophetic accountability is essential for healthy ministry. The prophet must be willing to submit their revelations to mature believers, trusted leaders, or spiritual mentors. Accountability protects the prophet from pride, error, and isolation.

Accountability includes:

- sharing prophetic impressions with pastors
- inviting feedback
- submitting words for review
- being willing to be corrected
- explaining prophetic processes humbly
- acknowledging uncertainty when necessary

The prepared prophet does not fear accountability; they embrace it. They understand that prophetic ministry is safest when connected to spiritual community.

11. PROPHETIC WORDS HAVE CONSEQUENCES

A prophetic word, even when spoken in obedience, carries weight. It can impact emotions, decisions, relationships, and faith journeys. Prophets must be aware of the consequences that come with delivering revelation.

A careless word can create:

- fear
- confusion
- discouragement
- false expectations
- relational strain

A faithful word can produce:

- healing
- direction
- peace
- restoration
- spiritual growth
- renewed hope

The prophet must deliver words with the awareness that their message carries spiritual impact.

12. PROPHETIC WORDS MUST BE TESTED BY THOSE WHO RECEIVE THEM

The responsibility of testing prophetic words does not rest solely on the prophet. The listener must also evaluate the message. Prophets should encourage receivers to:

- pray about the word
- test it with Scripture
- seek confirmation
- examine their own heart
- consult spiritual leadership
- wait for peace

Mature prophets invite testing because they value truth over ego. Testing does not insult the prophet; it honors the Lord.

13. SOME PROPHETIC WORDS ARE CONDITIONAL

Certain prophetic words depend on the obedience of the person receiving them. God may reveal what can happen, not necessarily what will happen. Prophets must communicate conditions clearly.

A conditional word may include phrases like:

- "If you obey..."
- "If you turn..."
- "If you remain faithful..."
- "If you take this step..."

Conditional words call people into alignment with God's will. They empower the listener to partner with the message.

14. PROPHETIC WORDS MUST ALWAYS REFLECT THE LOVE AND CHARACTER OF GOD

Above all, the prophetic must reveal the heart of God. Even when the message is corrective, the tone must be redemptive. Prophets do not use God's voice to attack people; they use God's voice to call people into life.

Prophetic words should produce:

- hope, not despair
- clarity, not confusion
- conviction, not condemnation
- encouragement, not humiliation

- direction, not disorientation

The character of God must be visible in the delivery, tone, and purpose of every prophetic word.

15. A MATURE PROPHET KNOWS WHEN GOD SAYS, "DO NOT SPEAK"

One of the most overlooked aspects of prophetic maturity is learning when not to speak. Not every revelation should be shared. Some are warnings meant for prayer. Some are personal insights for the prophet's growth. Some are intimate secrets between the prophet and God.

Silence can be obedience.

The prepared prophet understands that speaking is only half of the prophetic calling. The other half is restraint. A prophet who cannot remain silent will eventually mishandle sacred revelation.

CONCLUSION: STEWARDING THE SACRED ANATOMY OF GOD'S VOICE

A prophetic word is not simply spoken. It is carried, shaped, refined, and delivered. It is revelation from God's Spirit processed through the prophet's spirit and offered to humanity with reverence.

Understanding the anatomy of a prophetic word protects its purity and increases its impact. The prepared prophet recognizes that prophecy is holy, that revelation is weighty, and that the voice of God must be treated with reverence and humility.

When prophets understand the structure of revelation—its origin, its interpretation, its timing, its delivery, its purpose, and its accountability—they become trustworthy vessels who carry God's heart with clarity and confidence.

This is the prophetic maturity God is building in you.

7

Prophetic Accuracy and Integrity

Guarding the Purity of God's Voice

INTRODUCTION: THE WEIGHT OF SPEAKING ON BEHALF OF GOD

One of the greatest honors in the Christian life is the ability to hear and speak the voice of God. Yet with that honor comes a level of responsibility unlike any other spiritual assignment. When a prophet speaks, people listen with the expectation that God is addressing them. That expectation alone makes prophetic integrity essential. The prepared prophet understands that accuracy is not simply a matter of knowledge or giftedness—it is a matter of holiness, discipline, maturity, and humility.

Prophetic accuracy is not about being perfect; it is about being pure. It is impossible for human beings to be flawless, but it is entirely possible—and necessary—for them to be faithful. God does not demand perfection from His prophets, but He does demand honesty, integrity, and reverence for His voice.

This chapter examines how the prepared prophet protects the purity of prophetic ministry through intentional practices that ensure accuracy, humility, and integrity in every word spoken.

1. ACCURACY BEGINS WITH THE FEAR OF THE LORD

Prophetic integrity is rooted in the fear of the Lord. The fear of the Lord is not terror—it is reverence. It is the deep awareness that God's voice is sacred and must be handled carefully. A prophet who carries the fear of the Lord does not speak casually. They do not rush to prophesy. They do not release words to gain approval or influence. Instead, they carefully consider the weight of divine communication and treat every moment of revelation with holy caution.

When the fear of the Lord is present, the prophet becomes:

- more careful with their words,
- more humble in their approach,
- more prayerful in their preparation,
- more cautious in their interpretation,
- and more accountable in their delivery.

The fear of the Lord is the foundation for prophetic accuracy. Without it, zeal becomes recklessness, and gifting becomes dangerous.

2. ACCURACY REQUIRES A SPIRIT OF TRUTH

Accuracy is not only about correctly conveying information—it is about embodying truth in character, lifestyle, and speech. The Holy

Spirit is called the Spirit of Truth, and the prophet must reflect His nature. A prophet who lives truthfully will speak truthfully. Conversely, a prophet whose personal life is marked by dishonesty or hidden compromise will eventually distort revelation.

Integrity is not optional for prophetic ministry. It is essential. The prophet must cultivate truthfulness in:

- relationships,
- speech,
- motives,
- finances,
- private life,
- and ministry practices.

Truthful prophets make trustworthy vessels. When truth governs the heart, accuracy flows naturally.

3. EMOTIONAL MATURITY PROTECTS PROPHETIC ACCURACY

Prophets feel deeply, but feelings must never govern prophecy. Many inaccurate prophetic words arise not from deception but from ungoverned emotion. When a prophet is tired, anxious, discouraged, angry, or overly excited, their emotions can interfere with revelation.

Emotional maturity requires the prophet to:

- recognize when they are not in a healthy emotional state,
- avoid giving prophetic words when emotionally overwhelmed,
- separate personal feelings from spiritual impressions,
- resist the pressure to speak prematurely,
- and seek healing when emotional wounds distort perception.

A prophet cannot correctly interpret spiritual truths if their emotional lenses are clouded. Emotional stability protects prophetic clarity.

4. ACCURACY INCREASES THROUGH BIBLICAL GROUNDING

The Bible is the ultimate measure of prophetic authenticity. No prophetic revelation can supersede Scripture. No prophet is permitted to "hear" something that reverses God's written standards. As the prophet grows in biblical knowledge, their ability to interpret revelation accurately increases.

Biblical grounding helps the prophet:

- recognize false impressions,
- understand spiritual patterns,
- interpret symbolic dreams more clearly,
- avoid doctrinal error,
- and discern truth from deception.

The most mature prophets are not those with the most visions but those with the deepest Scriptural understanding. Prophetic gifting can make you impressive, but biblical grounding makes you safe.

5. PROPHETS MUST GUARD AGAINST PERSONAL BIAS

Personal bias is one of the greatest threats to prophetic accuracy. Bias can cause the prophet to subconsciously shape a word based on personal preference, relational loyalty, cultural influence, political views, or emotional attachment.

Personal bias can distort revelation in subtle ways:

- interpreting a word according to what the listener wants to hear,
- softening a corrective message out of fear of conflict,
- intensifying a warning out of personal frustration,
- or inserting personal opinion into divine revelation.

The prepared prophet must constantly examine the motives of their heart and ask God to reveal any internal biases that may interfere with purity. Prophetic ministry is safest when personal desire is fully surrendered.

6. ACCURACY INCREASES WHEN PROPHETS WAIT ON CONFIRMATION

One hallmark of maturity is the willingness to wait. Many inaccurate prophetic words come from a premature release. God may reveal something early, but that does not always mean it should be spoken immediately. The prophet must wait for confirmation, clarity, and timing.

Confirmation may come through:

- repeated impressions,
- Scripture that aligns with the word,
- peace settling in the spirit,
- wise counsel from leaders,
- or divine timing that becomes evident through circumstances.

The mature prophet does not rush revelation; they refine it. They understand that accuracy improves through patience.

7. PROPHETS MUST REMAIN TEACHABLE AND CORRECTABLE

No prophet, no matter how seasoned, is above correction. Prophetic accuracy is strengthened when prophets cultivate humility and surrounding accountability. A prophet who cannot be corrected cannot be trusted.

Teachable prophets:

- submit their revelations for review,
- welcome feedback,
- admit when they misunderstand,
- accept correction without offense,
- and learn from mistakes with maturity.

Accountability does not weaken prophetic authority—it strengthens it. Prophets who walk alone become vulnerable to deception. Prophets who remain teachable grow in purity and effectiveness.

8. INTEGRITY REQUIRES ADMITTING WHEN YOU ARE UNSURE

Prophetic integrity allows room for uncertainty. Some prophets feel pressured to always appear confident, but such pressure leads to error. A mature prophet understands that not every impression is clear. Not every dream carries a complete interpretation. Not every vision is meant to be spoken.

Integrity gives the prophet permission to say:

- "I'm not sure,"
- "This is what I sense but I need to pray more,"
- "I could be wrong about the timing,"
- or "I need additional confirmation."

Honesty protects the purity of prophetic ministry. People do not need prophets who pretend to know everything; they need prophets who are honest enough to acknowledge the limits of their understanding.

9. INTEGRITY REQUIRES OWNING MISTAKES

No prophet is perfect. Even the most seasoned prophets have moments when they misinterpret or misunderstand what they hear. What separates mature prophets from immature ones is the willingness to acknowledge mistakes.

When a prophecy does not come to pass, or when a revelation is later discovered to be inaccurate, the prophet must respond with humility. They should

- apologize for the error,
- clarify what was misunderstood,
- explain the lesson learned (when appropriate),
- seek counsel for growth,
- and remain committed to purity.

Owning mistakes builds trust. Denying mistakes destroys credibility and creates confusion. Prophets who refuse to acknowledge error become unfit for future revelation. God trusts the humble, not the prideful.

10. PROPHETS MUST RESIST THE PRESSURE TO PERFORM

In some church settings, there is immense pressure placed on prophetic people to deliver words on demand, prophesy dramatically, or produce revelation at every gathering. This pressure can tempt prophets to speak from their imagination, emotion, or assumption rather than from true revelation.

The prepared prophet must resist the urge to perform. Performance is the enemy of purity. The prophet must always remember that their role is not to entertain, impress, or satisfy expectations—it is to obey God.

If God is not speaking, the prophet must remain silent. Silence can be more prophetic than speech when the Spirit is not releasing revelation.

11. PROPHETS MUST AVOID THE TEMPTATION OF EXAGGERATION

Exaggeration is a form of dishonesty, even when done with good intentions. Adding dramatic details to increase the emotional impact of a prophetic word is a violation of integrity. The prophet must not:

- overstate what God said,
- dramatize the message,
- add details to make the word more impressive,
- or stretch the meaning of the revelation.

God does not need our embellishment. His words carry authority on their own. The prophet's task is to represent God faithfully, not theatrically.

12. ACCURACY REQUIRES CLARITY IN COMMUNICATION

Sometimes prophetic words are inaccurate not because the revelation was wrong, but because the delivery was unclear. The prophet must learn to communicate revelation in clear, understandable language.

This includes:

- explaining the context,
- distinguishing revelation from interpretation,
- identifying what was symbolic versus literal,
- expressing uncertainty when relevant,
- and avoiding overly mystical language that confuses listeners.

God does not hide truth in confusion; prophets must communicate in a way that brings light, not obscurity.

13. INTEGRITY REQUIRES PROTECTING CONFIDENTIALITY

Prophets often receive sensitive information about individuals, ministries, or situations. Integrity requires strict confidentiality. Prophetic revelation must never be used as gossip. Personal details revealed in prayer, prophecy, or counseling must be guarded with absolute discretion.

The prophet must ensure that private information remains private. Revelation is not a weapon; it is a stewardship. Misusing revelation destroys trust and dishonors God.

14. PROPHETS MUST AVOID MANIPULATIVE PROPHECY

Prophetic words must never be used to influence or coerce someone into making a decision that benefits the prophet or aligns with their personal preference. Manipulative prophecy includes:

- using spiritual authority to push personal agendas,
- giving directional words that benefit the prophet,
- speaking "thus says the Lord" to gain power over people,
- or creating fear to control behavior.

Such practices are spiritually abusive and completely incompatible with prophetic integrity. A prepared prophet speaks truthfully without manipulating outcomes.

15. THE PURE PROPHET POINTS PEOPLE TO GOD, NOT THEMSELVES

False prophets draw attention to themselves. True prophets draw attention to God. The mature prophet does not build a personality cult around their prophetic gift. They do not seek followers, admiration, or celebrity status. They are not seduced by applause.

Prophetic integrity requires the prophet to continually redirect people to God, His Word, and His Spirit—not to their own voice. The prophet must remain a servant, never allowing charisma or gifting to overshadow humility.

CONCLUSION: A PURE VOICE IN A COMPROMISED WORLD

Accuracy and integrity are not optional traits—they are the very essence of prophetic credibility. A prophet who speaks truthfully, humbly, biblically, and responsibly becomes a vessel God can trust with deeper revelation. A prophet who misuses the prophetic gift becomes a danger to themselves and to others.

The prepared prophet must guard the purity of God's voice with diligence. They must cultivate reverence, humility, emotional stability, biblical depth, accountability, and truthfulness. When these qualities shape the prophet's life, their words carry undeniable weight and their ministry remains trustworthy.

This is the calling of the prepared prophet:

to speak accurately, live honestly, obey completely, and reflect God faithfully.

8

❦

The Prophet's Emotional Health

Standing Strong Amid Spiritual Weight and Human Pressure

INTRODUCTION: THE PROPHETIC HEART BEARS MORE THAN WORDS

Every prophetic voice carries more than revelation—they carry weight. Prophets feel deeply, discern intensely, and experience spiritual burdens in ways that others may never understand. While the prophetic call is a divine honor, it can also create significant emotional strain if not handled with wisdom, balance, and intentional care. Emotional health is not a secondary concern for the prophet—it is a core requirement for longevity, accuracy, and relational stability.

Prophets who neglect emotional health become vulnerable to exhaustion, discouragement, bitterness, or burnout. But prophets who intentionally maintain emotional balance become resilient vessels capable of carrying God's heart without being crushed by the assignment.

This chapter explores the emotional world of the prophet—their vulnerabilities, challenges, strengths, and strategies for remaining spiritually powerful and emotionally stable.

1. PROPHETS FEEL DEEPLY BECAUSE THEY SEE DEEPLY

One defining characteristic of prophetic people is emotional depth. Prophets experience emotions intensely because their spiritual senses are heightened. They feel the grief of God over sin, the urgency of God for repentance, and the compassion of God for the broken. They sense spiritual atmospheres, discern hidden motives, and carry burdens that others overlook.

While this depth is a gift, it can also become overwhelming. Prophets must learn to manage emotional intensity so it does not control or destabilize them.

The prepared prophet learns to acknowledge emotional sensitivity as part of the prophetic call, not a flaw. God gave prophets deep emotional capacity so they can carry His heart, but that same capacity must be guarded for their well-being.

2. EMOTIONAL SENSITIVITY WITHOUT WISDOM LEADS TO INSTABILITY

Emotional depth is powerful when governed by wisdom, but dangerous when left unmanaged. Prophets who lack emotional discipline are at risk of:

- misinterpreting feelings as revelation,
- reacting to situations rather than responding through the Spirit,
- becoming easily offended or misunderstood,
- carrying unnecessary burdens,
- making decisions based on intensity rather than clarity,
- and allowing spiritual pressure to manifest as emotional chaos.

Emotional instability weakens prophetic accuracy. When the prophet's emotions dominate, the voice of God becomes harder to discern. Wisdom teaches prophets how to separate their own emotional experiences from the emotions God is communicating.

The mature prophet learns emotional regulation, not emotional suppression.

3. PROPHETS MUST ACKNOWLEDGE THEIR HUMANITY

One of the greatest emotional dangers for prophetic people is the belief that they must always appear strong, spiritual, or unshakeable. This mindset leads to internal isolation where prophets feel they cannot express weakness, sadness, fatigue, or confusion.

But prophets are human. They experience:

- disappointment,
- loneliness,
- insecurity,
- fear,
- frustration,
- temptation,
- and exhaustion.

God does not call prophets to perfection; He calls them to honesty. Suppressing emotion leads to emotional buildup, which eventually erupts in unhealthy ways. The mature prophet recognizes their humanity and seeks support, rest, and emotional expression when necessary.

4. EMOTIONAL HEALTH BEGINS WITH SELF-AWARENESS

Prophets must become students of their own emotional patterns. Self-awareness allows the prophet to identify when emotional pressure is rising and when they need to slow down, pray, rest, or seek counsel.

Self-aware prophets can identify:

- What triggers their emotional exhaustion
- Whether they are carrying too much spiritual weight
- When their boundaries are being violated
- When they are misinterpreting a burden as a personal problem
- When their inner tank is empty
- When they are ministering out of fatigue instead of strength

Awareness is the doorway to healing. Without it, prophets function blindly, reacting rather than responding, and surviving rather than thriving.

5. EMOTIONAL WOUNDS CAN DISTORT PROPHETIC CLARITY

Past wounds, unresolved conflict, childhood trauma, relational betrayal, rejection, or church hurt can profoundly influence a prophet's emotional and spiritual perception. A wounded prophet may hear clearly but interpret painfully. They may prophesy from fear, mistrust, or defensiveness without realizing it.

Prophets must allow God to heal their emotional wounds so they do not become filters through which revelation is distorted. Healing protects prophetic accuracy. It brings stability. It restores perspective.

The prepared prophet embraces healing, counseling if needed, healthy relationships, and honest reflection as part of their prophetic maturation.

6. PROPHETS MUST LEARN TO LAY DOWN WEIGHTS THEY WERE NEVER MEANT TO CARRY

Prophets are often burden-bearers. They intercede for others, sense spiritual battles, carry visions, and feel the concerns of God. However, not every burden is theirs to carry long-term. Emotional exhaustion often comes when prophets take ownership of burdens that God intended only for momentary intercession.

The prophet must learn the difference between:

a burden to carry and a burden to release
a call to intercede and a call to act
a weight from God and a weight from people
compassion and codependency

Prophets who never release spiritual burdens become overwhelmed by them. Emotional health requires the prophet to surrender weights at the feet of Jesus rather than internalizing them.

7. THE PROPHET MUST GUARD AGAINST DISCOURAGEMENT

Discouragement is one of the most common emotional battles prophets face. It comes through:

- unfulfilled expectations,
- misunderstanding from others,
- delayed promises
- spiritual warfare,
- lack of support,
- rejection,
- seasons of silence,
- and spiritual fatigue.

Discouragement attacks the prophet's identity and confidence. It whispers lies about inadequacy, futility, or failure. Discouragement must be recognized quickly before it becomes despair.

The prepared prophet combats discouragement through:

- consistent intimacy,
- honest confession to God,
- connection with healthy believers,
- meditation on Scripture,
- gratitude practices,
- prophetic reminders of calling,
- and intentional rest.

Discouragement is a temporary emotion—not a permanent identity.

8. PROPHETS OFTEN STRUGGLE WITH LONELINESS

The prophetic call can feel isolating because prophets see what others do not see and hear what others do not hear. They often sense spiritual realities before others perceive them, which can lead to feelings of being misunderstood or out of place.

Loneliness becomes dangerous when the prophet withdraws emotionally or spiritually. The prepared prophet must learn to build healthy, intentional relationships with people who value them beyond their gifting.

Loneliness is not a sign of prophetic greatness—it is a sign that the prophet needs community. Even the strongest prophets need companionship, friendship, and human connection.

9. PROPHETS MUST SET EMOTIONAL AND RELATIONAL BOUNDARIES

Because prophets care deeply, they can easily become overwhelmed by the emotional needs of others. Some people will seek the prophet constantly for advice, comfort, prophecy, or guidance. Without boundaries, the prophet becomes drained, resentful, or emotionally depleted.

Healthy boundaries include:

- limiting access to emotionally draining individuals,
- learning to say "no" without guilt,
- protecting time for rest and personal life,
- refusing to rescue everyone,
- avoiding emotional entanglement,
- and recognizing when people misuse prophetic sensitivity.

Boundaries are not unspiritual—they are essential for emotional survival.

10. PROPHETS MUST RECOGNIZE THE SIGNS OF EMOTIONAL BURNOUT

Burnout does not appear suddenly. It builds gradually through prolonged spiritual and emotional strain. Prophets must be vigilant in recognizing early signs such as:

- irritability,
- fatigue,
- lack of clarity,
- increased doubt,
- spiritual numbness,
- excessive isolation,
- inability to pray deeply,
- or loss of joy in ministry.

Burnout is not a sign of weakness—it is a signal that the prophet needs renewal. The mature prophet responds to these signs by seeking rest, restoration, and connection with God.

11. REST IS A SPIRITUAL DISCIPLINE, NOT A WEAKNESS

Many prophets struggle to rest because they are driven by spiritual urgency. They sense so much spiritually that they feel guilty for resting physically. But spiritual effectiveness depends on physical, emotional, and mental health.

Rest includes:

- sleeping well,
- taking Sabbath seriously,
- limiting overcommitment,
- stepping away from spiritual responsibility temporarily,
- enjoying peaceful activities,
- and allowing God to refresh the soul.

Rest is not disobedience—it is obedience. A rested prophet hears God better than an exhausted one.

12. PROPHETS MUST LEARN HEALTHY EXPRESSION OF EMOTION

Prophetic people sometimes suppress emotion because they fear appearing weak or unspiritual. But suppressed emotion becomes toxic. Emotional authenticity is part of prophetic maturity.

Healthy expression includes:

- journaling feelings,
- praying honestly,
- talking with trusted friends or mentors,
- acknowledging sadness, grief, or anger before God,
- and seeking healing rather than pretending.

God can handle every emotion a prophet feels. Emotional expression keeps the heart tender and the spirit sensitive.

13. PROPHETS NEED SAFE PEOPLE TO PROCESS WITH

Every prophetic person needs relationships where they can be fully transparent without fear of judgment or exploitation. Safe people help the prophet:

- process burdens,
- clarify emotions,
- recognize blind spots,
- receive encouragement,
- and remain grounded.

Safe relationships may include:

- spiritual mentors,
- emotionally healthy friends,
- pastors,
- counselors,
- or fellow prophetic voices.

Prophets stay emotionally healthy when they refuse to isolate and instead embrace supportive community.

14. A PROPHET'S SPOUSE AND FAMILY MUST BE PROTECTED

Prophetic people often unintentionally burden their families with spiritual pressure. A prophet must avoid:

- oversharing burdens that family members are not equipped to handle,
- becoming emotionally unavailable due to ministry demands,
- expecting family to interpret spiritual weight,

- or allowing spiritual warfare to create household tension.

Healthy prophets protect their family first. They do not sacrifice their home on the altar of ministry. Emotional health includes maintaining healthy roles within family life.

15. THE PROPHET MUST GUARD THEIR MIND

The prophet's mind is a battlefield. The combination of spiritual sensitivity and emotional depth makes the mind a target for:

- intrusive thoughts,
- spiritual attack,
- fear,
- mental fatigue,
- overthinking,
- and anxiety.

A healthy prophet guards their mind through:

- renewing it with Scripture,
- rejecting false thoughts,
- practicing stillness,
- using discernment to identify spiritual attack,
- and seeking help when necessary.

A clear mind supports clear revelation.

16. JOY STRENGTHENS THE PROPHET'S EMOTIONAL RESILIENCE

Prophets often carry heavy burdens, but they must also cultivate joy. Joy lifts spiritual weight. Joy restores emotional balance. Joy strengthens resilience. Joy reminds the prophet that God is not only a judge, a king, or a commander—He is also a loving Father who delights in His people.

Joy is not optional; it is spiritual strength. A joyful prophet is a stable prophet. The prepared prophet intentionally cultivates joy through worship, gratitude, relationships, and simple pleasures.

17. EMOTIONAL HEALTH PROTECTS PROPHETIC ACCURACY

When the prophet is emotionally overwhelmed, weary, or wounded, their prophetic clarity diminishes. Emotional health becomes a safeguard against misinterpretation, impulsive prophecy, or inaccurate delivery.

Emotionally healthy prophets:

- hear God clearly,
- interpret accurately,
- communicate wisely,
- avoid unnecessary offense,
- and honor God faithfully.

Emotional health strengthens prophetic ministry because it stabilizes the vessel through which revelation flows.

CONCLUSION: EMOTIONAL HEALTH IS PART OF PROPHETIC HOLINESS

Emotional health is not simply a psychological matter—it is a spiritual discipline. The prepared prophet understands that prophetic ministry requires emotional resilience, relational wisdom, and personal vulnerability. Prophets who steward their emotional health remain strong, clear, trustworthy, and effective.

When the prophet's heart is healthy, their prophetic voice becomes clearer. When their emotions are balanced, their discernment becomes sharper. When their soul is rested, their spirit becomes more receptive.

A prepared prophet is not just spiritually anointed—they are emotionally whole, mentally strong, relationally balanced, and inwardly stable.

This is what sustains prophetic calling for a lifetime.

9

Prophetic Courage

Speaking Truth in Hostile Environments

INTRODUCTION: THE PROPHET'S VOICE IS TESTED WHERE TRUTH IS UNWELCOME

Every prophet eventually discovers that the greatest challenge is not hearing God—it is speaking for Him in environments where truth is not welcome. Prophecy is not simply a spiritual gift; it is an act of courage. It requires a holy boldness that stands firm even when confronted by resistance, disbelief, hostility, or cultural pressure. The prophet must be prepared not only to deliver God's message but to endure the environment in which the message is received.

Prophetic courage is not loud or aggressive; it is steadfast, confident, and rooted in a deep trust in God. It is the courage to speak truth with love, conviction, and clarity, even when the cost is high.

Prophets do not merely confront sin—they confront systems, atmospheres, and spiritual forces that oppose righteousness.

This chapter explores how the prepared prophet cultivates the courage necessary to speak truth in hostile environments, confront darkness with wisdom, and maintain purity when surrounded by compromise.

1. PROPHETS MUST UNDERSTAND THAT TRUTH PROVOKES RESISTANCE

Prophets are often surprised when their messages encounter hostility, but this opposition should be expected. Truth disrupts. Truth confronts. Truth challenges mindsets, exposes deception, and shines light on what others prefer to keep hidden. Anytime truth enters an environment where falsehood has been comfortable, resistance arises.

The prophet must understand that:

- some will oppose truth because it confronts their sin,
- others will resist because truth threatens their influence,
- some will reject it because it disrupts their comfort,
- and others will misunderstand it because it challenges their tradition or worldview.

The presence of resistance does not indicate that the prophet is wrong; often it indicates they are right. The prepared prophet does not shrink back when truth is challenged but stands firm knowing that hostility often accompanies obedience.

2. PROPHETIC COURAGE COMES FROM CONVICTION, NOT PERSONALITY

People often assume that prophets are naturally bold, outspoken individuals, but prophetic courage does not originate in personality—it originates in conviction. Some prophets are introverted, quiet, gentle, or reflective by nature, and yet they carry extraordinary courage when delivering the word of the Lord. Others may be outwardly confident yet falter when asked to speak difficult truth.

Courage grows out of:

- the conviction that God has spoken,
- the assurance that God is present,
- the awareness of divine assignment,
- the reverence for God above people,
- and the inner confidence that obedience matters more than acceptance.

Conviction gives the prophet the strength to stand—even when their personality would prefer to retreat.

3. THE PROPHET MUST OVERCOME THE FEAR OF PEOPLE

One of the most crippling forces that undermine prophetic courage is the fear of people. This fear includes:

- fear of rejection,
- fear of criticism,
- fear of conflict,
- fear of misunderstanding,
- fear of losing relationships,
- fear of being labeled harsh or judgmental,

- or fear of being unpopular.

The fear of people silences prophets and dilutes truth. But the fear of the Lord strengthens prophets and amplifies truth. The prophet cannot be governed by the approval of people, because prophetic obedience requires emotional freedom from human opinion.

The prepared prophet must continually remind themselves:

"I answer to God. I speak for God. I trust God. I obey God. I fear God more than people."

This mindset produces supernatural courage.

4. PROPHETIC COURAGE REQUIRES WISDOM, NOT RECKLESSNESS

Courage is not recklessness. Prophets must not confuse boldness with impulsive confrontation or harsh delivery. True prophetic courage balances truth with wisdom, discernment, and compassion.

Wisdom teaches the prophet:

- when to speak and when to remain silent,
- where to speak and where not to speak,
- how to speak so that truth is received rather than resisted,
- and whom to speak to based on spiritual readiness.

A reckless prophet speaks without timing or discernment and creates unnecessary hostility. A wise prophet speaks when the moment is right, allowing truth to pierce the heart rather than provoke unnecessary offense.

Courage without wisdom becomes harmful.
Wisdom without courage becomes silent.

But when wisdom and courage unite, prophecy becomes transformative.

5. THE PROPHET MUST SPEAK WITH TRUTH AND LOVE

Prophetic courage is not expressed through aggression, intimidation, or condemnation. True courage speaks truth in love, even when the message is difficult. Love does not soften truth—it strengthens it. Love does not remove correction—it refines its purpose. Love does not avoid confrontation—it ensures confrontation leads to healing rather than humiliation.

Prophets must remember that the goal of prophecy is not to win arguments but to win hearts. When truth is spoken with arrogance, people shut down. When truth is spoken with compassion, people listen—even if the message is challenging.

Prophetic courage requires the prophet to carry the heart of God while delivering the words of God.

6. HOSTILE ENVIRONMENTS TEST, REFINE, AND STRENGTHEN THE PROPHET

Without resistance, prophetic courage cannot mature. Hostile environments shape the prophet by forcing them to rely on God for strength, clarity, and confidence. When the prophet faces pushback, it reveals:

- whether their identity is rooted in God,
- whether their convictions are stable,
- whether their motives are pure,
- whether their emotional health is strong,
- and whether their faith is fully developed.

Opposition does not destroy the prophet—it strengthens them. Every challenge becomes training. Every rejection becomes refinement. Every difficult assignment becomes preparation for greater influence.

7. PROPHETS MUST LEARN TO SPEAK TRUTH TO POWER

Many prophetic assignments require confronting people in positions of authority—leaders, pastors, political officials, business owners, or influential individuals. Speaking truth to power requires extraordinary courage because the consequences can be significant.

When facing authority, the prophet must:

- remain respectful,
- remain clear,
- remain humble,
- remain obedient,
- and remain grounded in God's voice.

Prophets do not confront power out of arrogance but out of obedience. Their posture should be one of reverence for God, not rebellion against leadership. When prophets speak with honor and truth simultaneously, their words carry undeniable authority.

8. PROPHETIC COURAGE MUST ENDURE MISUNDERSTANDING AND MISREPRESENTATION

Prophets are often misunderstood—not because they are unclear, but because their message challenges what others prefer to believe.

When prophets speak truth that confronts culture, spiritual systems. or personal sin, they may be misrepresented as:

- judgmental,
- divisive,
- too intense,
- overly spiritual,
- unloving,
- or disruptive.

Misrepresentation is painful, especially for emotionally sensitive prophets. But the prepared prophet does not allow misunderstanding to silence their voice. They trust that God understands what others cannot see.

A prophet's calling is not to be understood—it is to be obedient.

9. THE PROPHET MUST RESIST THE TEMPTATION TO RETREAT

After experiencing hostility, rejection, or criticism, many prophets are tempted to retreat into silence. They begin to avoid speaking truth to avoid conflict. They minimize their message to maintain peace They step back from prophetic responsibility to protect themselves emotionally.

This retreat may feel safe, but it is spiritually costly.

A silent prophet is not a peaceful prophet—they are a wounded one. Silence may protect the prophet temporarily, but it also deprives the world of the truth God entrusted to them. The prepared prophet must resist the temptation to withdraw and instead learn how to heal, regroup, and continue speaking truth.

10. PROPHETIC COURAGE REQUIRES A DEEP TRUST IN GOD'S PROTECTION

Prophets often confront spiritual forces, manipulative people, and hostile environments, yet their safety does not come from strategy alone—it comes from God's supernatural protection. The prophet must cultivate a continual awareness that:

- God goes before them,
- God shields them,
- God strengthens them,
- God fights for them,
- God preserves their voice,
- and God vindicates their obedience.

Prophetic assignments may place the prophet in uncomfortable—even dangerous—positions, but the prepared prophet speaks boldly because they trust the God who sent them.

11. PROPHETIC COURAGE REQUIRES CONFIDENCE IN IDENTITY

Prophets who doubt their calling will hesitate. Prophets who question their worth will remain silent. Prophets who feel insecure will compromise. But prophets who are confident in their identity will speak truth even when it is difficult.

Identity gives courage:

- "I am called by God."
- "I am chosen for this assignment."
- "I am anointed to speak truth."
- "I am protected by the Spirit."
- "I am equipped for this moment."

Courage grows when identity is secure. The prepared prophet must return continually to the roots of their calling to maintain confidence.

12. THE PROPHET MUST SPEAK TRUTH EVEN WHEN IT COSTS THEM

There will be moments when prophetic obedience costs something:

- relationships,
- popularity,
- respect,
- comfort,
- opportunities,
- or emotional peace.

Courage is tested not when prophecy is easy, but when prophecy is costly. The prophet must decide whether they value obedience over acceptance, truth over comfort, and fidelity to God over the favor of people.

The prepared prophet accepts the cost and remains faithful.

13. PROPHETIC COURAGE MUST BE ANCHORED IN HUMILITY

Courage without humility becomes pride. Humility without courage becomes fear. The prophet must embody both simultaneously. Humility keeps courage pure by reminding the prophet:

- that they are God's vessel, not God's equal,
- that they do not speak from superiority but from servanthood,
- that their authority comes from God alone,

- and that every word spoken is a sacred trust, not a personal achievement.

Humble courage is the posture through which God's voice is most accurately delivered.

14. PROPHETIC COURAGE GROWS THROUGH EXPERIENCE

The more the prophet obeys God in hostile environments, the stronger their courage becomes. Confidence grows each time the prophet witnesses God's faithfulness in challenging situations.

Experience teaches the prophet:

- that God speaks clearly,
- that God supports obedience,
- that truth transforms lives,
- that hostility is survivable,
- that rejection is not fatal,
- and that God's presence is constant.

Every act of obedience becomes a chapter in the prophet's training manual. Courage is not instant—it is accumulated.

15. PROPHETIC COURAGE MUST BE SUSTAINED BY PRAYER

Courage is not a personality trait but a spiritual strength produced in the place of prayer. When prophets spend time with God, fear weakens and boldness strengthens. Prayer gives the prophet:

- spiritual reinforcement,

- emotional grounding,
- renewed conviction,
- divine perspective,
- and unwavering resolve.

Prophets who pray boldly speak boldly.

CONCLUSION: COURAGE IS THE PROPHET'S MANTLE IN THE FACE OF RESISTANCE

Prophetic courage is not loud, reckless, or confrontational. It is steady, humble, resilient, and deeply rooted in obedience. The prepared prophet understands that hostility is not a sign of failure but a sign of the significance of their assignment. They speak truth with love, wisdom, and conviction even when the environment is resistant.

A prophet becomes truly prepared not when they hear God clearly, but when they obey Him courageously. This courage enables them to stand in boardrooms, pulpits, communities, nations, and spiritual battlegrounds with unwavering faithfulness.

This is the courage of the prepared prophet:

the courage to stand, to speak, to endure, and to remain faithful in every environment—hostile or receptive—until God's truth is heard.

10

The Prophet and the Local Church

Alignment, Accountability, and Spiritual Order

INTRODUCTION: THE PROPHET DOES NOT STAND ALONE

Contrary to popular belief, prophetic ministry was never designed to function in isolation. While prophets often carry unique burdens, unusual insight, and deep spiritual intensity, they are not exempt from the structure, fellowship, and accountability that God established within the local church. A prophet without a church covering becomes vulnerable. A church without prophetic ministry becomes incomplete.

The prepared prophet understands that the local church is not a restriction—it is a safeguard. It is not a limitation—it is a spiritual ecosystem through which the prophet matures, serves, receives support, and contributes to the overall health of the body of Christ Prophetic ministry thrives in environments where order, teamwork. humility, and mutual submission exist.

This chapter explores how prophets align with the local church. how they serve within spiritual authority, and how biblical order protects both the prophet and the congregation.

1. THE LOCAL CHURCH IS GOD'S DESIGN FOR SPIRITUAL GROWTH

The prophet must recognize that the local church is not a human invention—it is a divine blueprint. God created the church to be a spiritual family, a training environment, a place of discipleship, a community of accountability, and a center of spiritual activation

Prophets grow best in environments where:

- worship is continual,
- teaching is grounded,
- fellowship is authentic,
- prayer is consistent,
- and leadership is accountable.

The prophetic gift becomes dangerous when separated from the church because isolation makes the prophet susceptible to pride, error, imbalance, and emotional strain. God never intended for prophets to function as independent spiritual freelancers. They are part of Christ's body, and they must remain connected to the body.

2. PROPHETS MUST HONOR SPIRITUAL AUTHORITY

Every healthy church has spiritual authority—pastors, elders, overseers, and leaders who guide the congregation. Prophets are not above this order. They do not operate in their own spiritual jurisdiction. They serve under pastoral covering.

Honoring spiritual authority does not diminish the prophetic—it strengthens it. A prophet who submits to authority displays maturity and humility, demonstrating that they can function within God's structure.

Submission includes:

- respecting leadership even when not fully understood,
- seeking permission before releasing sensitive words publicly,
- avoiding undermining pastoral leadership,
- acknowledging that pastors are accountable for the flock,
- and partnering with leadership rather than competing with them.

Spiritual authority is not dominance—it is safety. Prophets flourish under pastors who value the prophetic and protect the congregation simultaneously.

3. PROPHETS MUST FUNCTION WITHIN SPIRITUAL ORDER

Biblical prophetic ministry is always relational, orderly, and accountable. Disorder does not indicate freedom—it reveals immaturity. Prophets must avoid operating impulsively, unpredictably, or without structure. The Holy Spirit moves powerfully through order.

Prophetic order includes:

- receiving permission before ministering publicly,
- following church protocols for prophetic words,
- respecting time, environment, and flow of service,
- aligning with the vision and culture of the church,
- and allowing leadership to discern when and how words should be released.

When the prophet embraces order, their ministry becomes a blessing rather than a disruption.

4. PROPHETS MUST SUPPORT THE VISION OF THE HOUSE

Every local church carries a unique vision. Prophets must align with that vision rather than creating their own parallel agenda. Prophets are not called to build personal kingdoms—they are called to strengthen God's Kingdom through unity.

A prophet strengthens the house when they:

- serve faithfully within church ministries,
- speak words that reinforce the church's spiritual direction,
- encourage the body to follow pastoral leadership,
- pray consistently for the church's mission,
- and avoid creating personal followers or factions.

The prophet who supports the vision becomes a powerful asset to the church's spiritual health.

5. PROPHETS ARE CALLED TO EDIFY, NOT CONTROL

Prophets must be careful not to assume a controlling or domineering posture within the congregation. Their role is to edify, encourage, and strengthen—not to police, intimidate, or dominate.

Prophets edify the church by:

- offering timely encouragement,
- calling people into alignment with God's will,
- interceding for spiritual needs,
- releasing clarity when confusion rises,
- and supporting believers during seasons of transition.

They must avoid:

- correcting everyone they see,
- confronting church members harshly,
- assuming authority without permission,
- or speaking authoritatively where God has not spoken.

Prophets are servants, not spiritual dictators. The prepared prophet uses their authority to uplift, not to overpower.

6. PROPHETS MUST DISTINGUISH BETWEEN PERSONAL BURDENS AND CORPORATE WORDS

Prophets often sense things personally that are not meant for public release. Some prophetic impressions are for private intercession. Others are for pastoral leadership alone. Some are for personal reflection. A wise prophet discerns the difference.

The prophet must ask:

- "Is this for me?"
- "Is this for leadership?"
- "Is this for intercession?"
- "Is this for the congregation?"
- "Is this for the future?"

When prophets release private burdens publicly, confusion follows. When they share corporate words privately, impact is lost. Discernment ensures words are delivered in the right context.

7. PROPHETS AND PASTORS ARE PARTNERS, NOT OPPONENTS

One of the enemy's greatest strategies is to divide prophets from pastors. Prophets tend to be visionary, sensitive, and future-oriented, while pastors tend to be nurturing, protective, and stability-oriented. These differences are complementary, not contradictory.

When pastors and prophets partner:

- churches gain clarity and protection,
- the congregation grows in maturity,
- spiritual balance is maintained,
- revelation and wisdom flow together,
- and the church moves in both power and order.

Prophets must not view pastors as obstacles to revelation. Pastors must not view prophets as threats to stability. Together, they create a healthy spiritual ecosystem.

8. PROPHETS MUST MAINTAIN A TEACHABLE SPIRIT IN THE CHURCH

Maturity requires humility. Prophets must remain teachable under local church leadership. Being prophetic does not make a person omniscient. They must still learn, grow, receive correction, and submit to discipleship.

A teachable prophet:

- listens when leadership provides counsel,
- receives correction without offense,
- practices humility in community settings,
- avoids spiritual arrogance,
- and values the wisdom of seasoned believers.

Teachable prophets become trustworthy prophets. Unteachable prophets become dangerous.

9. PROPHETS MUST AVOID CREATING DIVISION OR FACTIONS

Because prophets carry intense passion, some people gravitate toward them, forming emotional or spiritual attachments. If not managed wisely, prophets can unintentionally create "prophetic cliques," where members prefer their insights over pastoral leadership.

Division can emerge when:

- people seek prophecy more than discipleship,
- prophets allow followers to elevate them,
- church members bypass leadership to seek prophetic direction,
- or prophets begin to function independently.

The prepared prophet directs all attention to Christ, not themselves. They uphold unity at all costs and direct people back to pastoral authority.

10. THE PROPHET'S ROLE IS TO CONFIRM, NOT REPLACE, GOD'S VOICE TO INDIVIDUALS

Some believers expect prophets to make decisions for them. They want direction about career choices, relationships, finances, or personal matters. While God may occasionally give prophets insight into someone's path, prophecy should confirm what God is already speaking—not replace their personal relationship with Him.

Prophets must avoid becoming:

- spiritual crutches.
- personal advisors on demand,
- substitutes for the Holy Spirit,
- or decision-makers for people's private lives.

Prophecy strengthens believers. It does not make them dependent. Healthy prophetic ministry activates spiritual growth rather than creating unhealthy reliance.

11. PROPHETS ARE ESSENTIAL TO CHURCH INTERCESSION

Prophets carry unique spiritual sensitivity, making them powerful intercessors within the church. Their prayers often address unseen battles, upcoming challenges, or spiritual attacks before anyone else recognizes them.

Prophets enrich the church's prayer life by:

- praying strategically,
- sensing spiritual atmospheres during worship,
- discerning demonic activity,
- providing prophetic insight for prayer teams,
- and covering pastoral leadership in targeted intercession.

The prophet who prays for the church becomes a pillar of spiritual protection.

12. PROPHETS MUST BE INTEGRATED INTO MINISTRY TEAMS

Rather than functioning on the fringes, prophets should be integrated into the church's ministry structure. This integration might include:

- advisory roles to pastors,
- prophetic insight for leadership meetings,
- participation in prayer teams,
- spiritual counsel for ministry leaders,
- or occasional prophetic teaching or training.

Integration prevents isolation. It gives the prophetic gift a healthy place to flourish. It also ensures accountability and alignment.

13. PROPHETS MUST EXERCISE PATIENCE WITH THE CHURCH'S PACE

Prophets often see things far in advance. Their vision is ahead of the congregation's readiness. This can create frustration if the prophet expects immediate change.

The prophet must recognize that:

- the church moves at a pastoral pace, not a prophetic pace,
- people grow gradually, not instantly,
- culture shifts over time,
- and timing must match spiritual maturity.

Patience protects the prophet's heart from resentment and prevents relational conflict. Prophets who lack patience often misinterpret slow movement as resistance, when it may simply be God's timing.

14. PROPHETS MUST AVOID REACTING WHEN THEIR WORDS ARE NOT IMMEDIATELY RECEIVED

A prophet may share a word that leadership does not immediately implement or even agree with. When this happens, the prophet must remain secure and humble. Not every word requires immediate action. Leadership may need confirmation, clarity, or additional insight.

The prophet must resist:

- offense,
- frustration,
- withdrawal,
- spiritual superiority,
- or bitterness.

Submission to timing is part of prophetic maturity.

15. PROPHETS STRENGTHEN THE UNITY AND PURITY OF THE CHURCH

When functioning properly, prophets bring:

- spiritual clarity,
- increased discernment,
- deeper worship,
- stronger prayer culture,
- heightened awareness of spiritual warfare,
- revival atmosphere,
- and alignment with God's will.

Prophets help keep the church spiritually awake, alert, and sensitive to the movement of the Spirit. They ensure the congregation does not drift from God's heart or divine assignment.

The church becomes stronger when prophets operate in humility and cooperation.

CONCLUSION: THE LOCAL CHURCH IS THE PROPHET'S SPIRITUAL HOME

The prepared prophet understands that God designed the church as a place of community, order, accountability, and mutual support. The prophet and the church need each other. The prophet brings clarity, revelation, and spiritual depth. The church provides grounding, protection, structure, and relational balance.

When prophets embrace the local church, their gift matures. Their voice gains credibility. Their ministry becomes safe, effective, and fruitful. Their calling integrates into the broader body of Christ, where it can thrive for a lifetime.

This is the posture of the prepared prophet—
humble under authority,
aligned with spiritual order,
accountable within community,
and committed to strengthening the church God loves.

11

Prayer as Prophetic Warfare

Intercession, Travail, and the Fight for God's Will

INTRODUCTION: THE PROPHET'S BATTLEGROUND IS THE PLACE OF PRAYER

The prophet's greatest victories are not won in public—they are won in private. Long before a prophetic word is spoken, and long after it is delivered, the prophet stands in the trenches of prayer. Prophetic ministry is not only about revelation; it is about warfare. The prophet sees what others do not see, discerns what others overlook, and feels spiritual pressure before it becomes visible. Because of this, prophets must become warriors in prayer, equipped to push back darkness, intercede for God's people, and contend for the fulfillment of divine purpose.

Prayer is not a preparation for the battle.
Prayer is the battle.

Every prophetic word must be conceived in prayer, carried through prayer, and protected in prayer. Prophets are not spectators in spiritual warfare—they are frontline soldiers. They receive battle plans from Heaven and carry them out on earth. They intercede for families, churches, regions, and nations. They confront demonic assignments through the authority of Christ. They pray with fervency, perseverance, and spiritual precision.

This chapter examines the essential role of prayer in prophetic life and reveals why prophets must become skilled in intercession and spiritual warfare.

1. PROPHETS CANNOT FUNCTION WITHOUT A DEEP PRAYER LIFE

The prophetic and prayer are inseparable. Every prophet in Scripture was a person of deep prayer. Moses interceded for Israel until God changed His mind. Elijah prayed until rain returned to a barren land. Daniel prayed three times a day despite threats to his life. Anna prayed for decades before Christ's arrival. The early church prophets prayed, fasted, and ministered to the Lord before receiving direction.

Why is prayer essential for the prophet?

- It keeps the heart aligned with God's heart.
- It clears spiritual clutter so revelation becomes clear.
- It strengthens discernment.
- It purifies motives and attitudes.
- It sustains emotional health.
- It protects the prophet from deception.
- It activates spiritual authority.
- It replenishes the prophet after spiritual assignment.

Prophets without prayer become gifted but dangerous. Prophets anchored in prayer become accurate, stable, and effective.

2. PROPHETS INTERCEDE BECAUSE THEY CARRY INSIGHT OTHERS DO NOT

One of the primary functions of a prophet is intercession. Prophets stand between Heaven and earth, between God and people, between crisis and breakthrough. Because prophets see spiritual danger ahead of time, they must pray proactively rather than reactively.

Intercession is not simply praying for needs—it is spiritual partnership with God. It is the prophet saying:

"Lord, I will carry the burden You've shown me until You release it."

Prophetic intercession includes:

- praying until a spiritual heaviness lifts,
- praying until clarity comes,
- praying until a burden transforms into peace,
- praying until demonic assignments break,
- praying until breakthrough emerges.

Intercessors pray from compassion; prophets pray from revelation Both are essential, but prophetic intercession carries a unique strategic dimension.

3. PROPHETS ENGAGE IN TRAVAIL: THE DEEP GROANING OF THE SPIRIT

Travail is one of the most intense forms of prophetic prayer. It is not emotional breakdown—it is spiritual birthing. Travail often manifests as groaning, weeping, trembling, or deep burden that cannot be expressed in ordinary words. It is the Spirit praying through the prophet for something God desires to birth in the earth.

Travail happens when:

- revail is near,
- breakthrough is pending,
- someone's deliverance is imminent,
- a church is on the brink of spiritual transformation,
- or a nation is entering spiritual crisis.

Travail cannot be manufactured; it is produced by the Spirit. When the prophet yields to travail, they participate in the birthing of God's will.

4. PROPHETIC PRAYER EXPOSES AND CONFRONTS THE WORKS OF DARKNESS

Because prophets see in the spirit, they must be prepared for warfare. Demonic opposition intensifies whenever prophetic revelation increases. Prophets often discern:

- attacks on individuals,
- generational patterns,
- hidden sin,
- witchcraft assignments,
- territorial spirits,
- spiritual influences over regions,

- or demonic interference in churches.

When the prophet senses such activity, they must confront it through spiritual warfare—not fear, not avoidance, not silence.

Prophetic warfare includes:

- declaring Scripture against demonic lies,
- commanding darkness to flee in Jesus 'name,
- breaking generational strongholds,
- praying over atmospheres,
- resisting spiritual intimidation,
- and enforcing the victory of the Cross.

Prophets fight battles few others know exist.

5. PROPHETS MUST PRAY FOR PASTORS AND LEADERS

Prophetic and pastoral ministries are deeply connected. Prophets often discern the spiritual attacks and pressures that leaders face. Because of this, they are uniquely positioned to intercede for leadership.

Prophets must pray:

- for their pastor's integrity,
- for their pastor's emotional strength,
- for their pastor's marriage and family,
- for wisdom in decision-making,
- for protection from spiritual attack,
- for unity within leadership teams.

A prophet who does not pray for leadership cannot effectively support or correct leadership. Intercession is the prophet's act of loyalty, protection, and spiritual alignment.

6. PROPHETS MUST PRAY INTO THE WORDS THEY RELEASE

A prophetic word does not end when it is spoken. Some words require ongoing prayer to bring them into fulfillment. Prophets must steward their words in prayer by:

- revisiting them regularly,
- praying over them,
- asking God for timing,
- seeking clarity for the next steps,
- resisting discouragement when fulfillment is delayed,
- and standing against demonic resistance that attempts to hinder the word.

Prophetic words are seeds. Prayer is water. Without prayer, prophetic words remain dormant.

7. PRAYER PROTECTS THE PROPHET FROM EMOTIONAL AND SPIRITUAL EXHAUSTION

Prophets experience intense pressure because of their spiritual sensitivity. Prayer becomes the place where the prophet releases burdens, restores strength, and regains clarity. Without prayer, prophets become:

- overwhelmed,
- anxious,
- frustrated,

- emotionally drained,
- spiritually confused,
- or vulnerable to attack.

Prayer is not only a weapon—it is medicine. It heals the heart, calms the spirit, and renews the mind. A prophet who neglects prayer becomes spiritually fragile. A prophet who prioritizes prayer becomes spiritually unshakeable.

8. PROPHETS MUST PRAY WITH AUTHORITY, NOT PASSIVITY

Prophets are called to pray with spiritual authority. Authority is demonstrated when the prophet understands their identity, position in Christ, and the power of the Spirit within them. Prophetic authority avoids timid, hesitant praying. It is confident, clear, scripturally grounded, and empowered by faith.

Authoritative prayer includes:

- declaring God's promises,
- commanding spiritual resistance to break,
- praying boldly for healing or deliverance,
- speaking God's will into the earth,
- confronting lies with truth,
- and releasing heaven's agenda with faith.

Authority is not arrogance—it is obedience.

9. PROPHETS MUST PRAY STRATEGICALLY, NOT RANDOMLY

Because prophets see spiritually, they are not called to pray general prayers alone. Prophetic prayer is strategic. It targets specific assignments, atmospheres, and circumstances.

Strategic prophetic prayer may include:

- praying for specific people under attack,
- breaking demonic patterns in certain families,
- releasing clarity for church vision,
- confronting spiritual apathy,
- addressing national or regional issues,
- praying for the advancement of God's kingdom in specific areas.

A strategic prayer life increases prophetic precision and multiplies effectiveness.

10. PROPHETS MUST DISCERN THE SOURCE OF SPIRITUAL BURDEN

Not every spiritual heaviness is from God. Prophets must discern:

- spiritual burden from the Holy Spirit,
- emotional heaviness from personal stress,
- demonic oppression from the enemy,
- compassion from human empathy,
- and intercessory prompting from divine assignment.

Misreading the source of a burden leads to confusion. When the prophet discerns correctly, they pray effectively.

11. PROPHETS MUST PRACTICE PERSISTENT PRAYER

Some spiritual battles require persistence. Not every breakthrough comes instantly. Prophetic intercession may last:

- hours,
- days,
- months,
- or even years.

Persistence does not mean doubt; it means commitment. Persistence is how prophetic promises are birthed. The prophet must fight through:

- discouragement,
- spiritual fatigue,
- silence,
- resistance,
- and delays.

Breakthrough belongs to those who persevere.

12. PROPHETS MUST PRAY FOR PROTECTION FROM SPIRITUAL ATTACK

Prophets are targets. Their insight threatens the enemy. Their words shift atmospheres. Their prayers weaken demonic structures. Because of this, prophets must pray regularly for protection.

Protection includes prayer over:

- the mind,

- the emotions,
- the heart,
- the home,
- the marriage,
- the children,
- the finances,
- the ministry.

Prophetic covering is not optional—it is necessary.

13. PROPHETIC WARFARE MUST BE BALANCED WITH REST IN GOD'S PRESENCE

Prophets can become so focused on warfare that they forget to rest. But warfare is only effective when balanced with worship, intimacy, and peace. Rest does not diminish authority; it strengthens it.

Rest in God includes:

- worship without agenda,
- quietness before the Lord,
- listening without striving,
- enjoying God's presence,
- allowing God to minister back to the prophet.

Rest prevents burnout and restores spiritual clarity. Prophets fight better when they rest well.

14. PROPHETIC WARFARE MUST ALWAYS BE ROOTED IN LOVE

Prophets do not fight out of anger or pride—they fight because they love God and love people. Their warfare is grounded in compassion, not frustration. They intercede because they care. They confront darkness because they desire to see people free. They travail because they long for God's agenda to manifest.

The weapon of the prophet is not aggression; it is love.

15. PROPHETS MUST REMEMBER THAT PRAYER CHANGES THEM FIRST

Prophetic prayer transforms situations, but it also transforms the prophet. As they pray, God purifies motives, strengthens faith, deepens character, and refines discernment. The prophet emerges from prayer not only as a warrior but as a vessel shaped by intimacy.

The greatest victories of a prophet are internal before they become external.

CONCLUSION: PROPHETIC PRAYER IS THE FURNACE WHERE GOD FORMS HIS WARRIORS

Prophets cannot walk in their calling without becoming masters of prayer. Intercession, travail, warfare, silence, listening, and strategic prayer form the spiritual backbone of prophetic ministry. Prophets are not defined merely by what they say—they are defined by how they pray.

The prepared prophet carries the heart of God into the battleground of intercession. They push back darkness, birth purpose, protect the church, support leadership, and enforce God's will through prayer. This is not optional. It is essential.

Every prophetic victory begins with bowed knees, burning hearts, and unshakeable faith.

This is the warfare of the prepared prophet—
to pray until heaven moves,
to intercede until breakthrough comes,

to travail until purpose is born,
and to stand until God's will prevails.

12

Prophetic Character

The Inner Life That Sustains the Outer Call

INTRODUCTION: CHARACTER IS THE PROPHET'S TRUE ANOINTING

In prophetic ministry, gifting may open a door, but character keeps it open. Revelation may draw an audience, but integrity sustains influence. Accuracy may impress people, but humility pleases God. The greatness of a prophet is not measured by how many visions they see or how many words they deliver. It is measured by the strength of their inner life—who they are when no one is watching, listening, applauding, or affirming.

Character is not optional for the prophet.
It is essential.
It is not secondary—it is foundational.

Prophetic ministry becomes dangerous when character is shallow but gifting is deep.

The prepared prophet learns early that God is more interested in shaping their heart than showcasing their gift. This chapter explores the inner traits necessary to sustain prophetic calling, safeguard integrity, and honor God through a life of holiness, humility, and emotional maturity.

1. CHARACTER PROTECTS THE PROPHET FROM THE DANGERS OF THEIR OWN GIFT

The prophetic gift is powerful. It can influence hearts, shape decisions, expose hidden realities, and alter spiritual trajectories. Without character, that power becomes risky. A prophet who lacks self-awareness, discipline, or humility may unintentionally use their gift recklessly—harming others and harming themselves.

Character protects the prophet from:

- pride,
- deception,
- manipulation,
- spiritual imbalance,
- unchecked authority,
- emotional instability,
- and moral compromise.

Gifting without character is like fire without containment—bright but destructive. Character gives the prophet roots, boundaries, and stability so the gift remains pure.

2. HUMILITY IS THE PROPHET'S MARK OF AUTHENTICITY

Humility is the most important character trait a prophet can possess. Prophets who remain humble are teachable, safe, and trusted. They do not see themselves as superior but as servants of God's purposes. They do not exalt their revelation but exalt the God who revealed it.

Humility protects the prophet by reminding them that:

- they are not the source of revelation—God is,
- they are not infallible,
- they must remain teachable and correctable,
- they cannot take credit for what only God can do,
- and their role is to serve, not dominate.

Humility anchors the prophet in truth. Pride pulls them into delusion. A humble prophet will never fall far because their heart remains grounded in obedience rather than applause.

3. INTEGRITY IS THE PROPHET'S SHIELD AGAINST CORRUPTION

Integrity means consistency between inner life and outer life—between what the prophet says and who the prophet is. Integrity protects the prophet from moral failure by requiring them to walk in honesty, transparency, and righteousness.

Integrity includes:

- telling the truth when it is difficult,
- honoring commitments,
- refusing to manipulate situations,

- maintaining sexual purity,
- handling money ethically,
- treating people with honor,
- and living above reproach.

A prophet with integrity does not hide behind the gift. They display the same character at home, at church, at work, and in private. Integrity builds lasting credibility.

4. PURITY IS THE PROPHET'S FOUNDATION FOR CLARITY

Purity strengthens prophetic accuracy. Sin dulls spiritual hearing. Compromise damages discernment. Hidden sin creates static in spiritual communication. The prophet must aggressively guard purity to maintain clarity.

Purity includes:

- pure motives,
- pure thoughts,
- pure speech,
- pure relationships,
- pure desires,
- and pure conduct.

Purity is not about perfection; it is about repentance, discipline, and consistently choosing righteousness. A pure prophet hears God clearly because their heart is not cluttered with hidden guilt or spiritual distraction.

5. EMOTIONAL MATURITY SUSTAINS PROPHETIC RESPONSIBILITY

Prophets are emotional beings. They feel with depth. They discern atmospheres. They sense spiritual pressure. Without emotional maturity, these traits become overwhelming. Emotional maturity ensures that the prophet can manage:

- frustration,
- discouragement,
- rejection,
- conflict,
- disappointment,
- and spiritual heaviness.

Emotionally mature prophets do not lash out, withdraw, or react impulsively. They remain grounded, patient, self-controlled, and wise. Emotional maturity keeps prophetic authority from becoming emotional instability.

6. SELF-DISCIPLINE SHAPES THE PROPHET INTO A VESSEL GOD CAN TRUST

Discipline is the prophet's training ground. Prophetic gifting alone is not enough—discipline strengthens the prophet's life so they can carry spiritual weight. Self-discipline ensures consistency in:

- prayer,
- fasting,
- study,
- time management,
- financial stewardship,
- and personal boundaries.

Undisciplined prophets eventually burn out, fall into deception, or misuse their gift. Disciplined prophets develop endurance, consistency, and credibility.

God gives revelation to anyone, but He entrusts influence to the disciplined.

7. ACCOUNTABILITY PROTECTS THE PROPHET FROM BLIND SPOTS

Every prophet has blind spots. Without accountability, these blind spots become spiritual pitfalls. Accountability is not a sign of weakness—it is a sign of maturity. The prepared prophet invites oversight, correction, and counsel.

Accountability includes:

- mentors who speak honestly,
- pastors who provide oversight,
- friends who offer emotional support,
- spiritual peers who give balanced perspective.

A prophet who rejects accountability becomes a danger to themselves and others. But a prophet who embraces accountability grows in humility, safety, and accuracy.

8. PATIENCE STRENGTHENS THE PROPHET'S ABILITY TO WAIT ON GOD

Prophets often see things long before others do. Because of this, they experience frustration when things happen slower than expected. Patience is essential because prophetic timing is rarely immediate.

Patience teaches the prophet:

- not to force fulfillment,
- not to manipulate outcomes,
- not to rush interpretation,
- not to push people prematurely,
- not to speak before clarity arrives,
- and not to assume God is late.

Patience protects the prophet from emotional impulsiveness and spiritual presumption.

9. FORGIVENESS KEEPS THE PROPHET'S HEART CLEAN

Prophets face rejection, misunderstanding, misjudgment, and spiritual attack. If they do not practice forgiveness, bitterness will take root. Bitterness poisons prophetic perception. It clouds discernment and hardens the heart.

Forgiveness includes:

- releasing people from emotional debt,
- refusing to carry offense,
- praying for those who hurt them,
- avoiding gossip and retaliation,
- and healing rather than hardening.

A forgiving prophet remains sensitive to God.
A bitter prophet becomes spiritually toxic.

10. COMPASSION IS THE PROPHET'S BRIDGE TO PEOPLE

Prophets deliver truth, but truth must be wrapped in compassion. Pure prophets do not enjoy correction. They weep over the broken, intercede for the rebellious, and pray for those who are hurting.

Compassion keeps the prophet from becoming:

- harsh,
- self-righteous,
- impatient,
- judgmental,
- or detached.

Compassion does not weaken the word—it softens the heart so the word can be received.

11. WISDOM GUIDES THE PROPHET'S DELIVERY, TIMING, AND TONE

Wisdom is one of the greatest gifts a prophet can possess. It helps them know:

- what to say,
- when to say it,
- how to say it,
- who to say it to,
- and when not to say anything at all.

Wisdom is the fence around the prophetic gift. Without it, truth can become harmful. With it, truth becomes transformative.

Prophetic wisdom grows through:

- Scripture,
- experience,
- prayer,
- mentorship,
- and humility.

Wisdom protects the prophet from recklessness.

12. CONTENTMENT KEEPS THE PROPHET FROM CHASING VALIDATION

Many prophetic people struggle with a desire for recognition. They want their gift to be affirmed. They want their voice to be heard. But the prepared prophet understands that contentment is essential.

Contentment means:

- resting in God's timing,
- embracing hidden seasons,
- refusing to compare calling with others,
- avoiding jealousy of other ministers,
- and trusting God to open doors.

A content prophet is focused on obedience rather than platform. They do not manipulate opportunities or demand visibility. They allow God to promote them in His time.

13. INTEGRITY IN RELATIONSHIPS KEEPS THE PROPHET GROUNDED

Prophets must maintain healthy relationships. Poor relational habits damage credibility and silence the prophetic voice. Healthy relationships require:

- respect,
- honesty,
- reliability,
- boundaries,
- and compassion.

Prophets cannot treat people as ministry assignments alone. They must value relationships for the sake of community, not usefulness. Healthy relationships anchor the prophet's humanity and emotional balance.

14. THE PROPHET MUST CULTIVATE A LIFESTYLE OF REPENTANCE

Repentance is not just for sinners—it is a daily posture for prophets. Repentance keeps the prophet's heart soft, humble, and available to God.

Repentance includes:

- confessing wrong thoughts or motives,
- addressing pride or jealousy,
- turning from unhealthy habits,
- acknowledging sin quickly,
- and welcoming spiritual cleansing.

Repentance is the maintenance of holiness. It keeps the prophet spiritually sharp, emotionally stable, and relationally healthy.

15. TEACHABILITY KEEPS THE PROPHET FROM BECOMING ARROGANT

Prophets must remain lifelong learners. No one outgrows growth. No one graduates from humility. Teachability ensures the prophet stays balanced, open, and correctable.

Teachability includes:

- learning from pastors,
- learning from Scripture,
- learning from mentors,
- learning through mistakes,
- learning through seasons of silence,
- and learning through God's correction.

A teachable prophet is a safe prophet.
A proud prophet becomes a liability.

CONCLUSION: CHARACTER IS THE PROPHET'S TRUE CALLING

The prepared prophet understands that character is not optional—it is the backbone of prophetic ministry. Without character, revelation becomes reckless. Without integrity, influence becomes dangerous. Without humility, gifting becomes corrupted.

The prophet God prepares is not only accurate in hearing but trustworthy in living. Their life reflects the message they carry. Their heart remains clean. Their motives remain pure. Their obedience remains consistent. Their relationships remain healthy. Their voice remains credible.

This is the character of the prepared prophet:
rooted, stable, humble, disciplined, pure, accountable, wise, and teachable.

This is the inner life that sustains the outer call.
This is the maturity that keeps the prophet safe.
This is the holiness that honors the God who speaks.

13

Hearing God Clearly

*Discerning the Shepherd's Voice in a
Noisy World*

INTRODUCTION: THE PROPHET'S PRIMARY
ASSIGNMENT IS TO HEAR

For all the prophetic assignments a prophet may receive—intercession, exhortation, correction, visions, warnings, confirmations, and anointed declarations—none is more critical than learning to hear God clearly. Every prophetic action flows from this one core competency. If the prophet cannot distinguish God's voice from their own thoughts, emotions, fears, desires, or external influences, every other part of the prophetic life becomes unstable.

The world today is louder than ever. Countless voices compete for attention—social media, culture, politics, religion, personal ambition, spiritual noise, emotional impulses, and even the expectations of others. In such an environment, hearing God becomes both a discipline and a miracle. The prophet must learn to cultivate inner quietness, sharpen spiritual sensitivity, and develop discernment so that God's whisper becomes unmistakable.

Hearing God is not accidental. It is intentional. It is not mystical. It is relational. It is not reserved for the elite. It is accessible to every believer—but prophets are called to master it.

This chapter explores how the prepared prophet hears God clearly, even in a world overflowing with noise.

1. HEARING GOD BEGINS WITH RELATIONSHIP, NOT TECHNIQUE

Many people desire formulas for hearing God, but prophetic clarity begins in relationship, not ritual. God speaks most clearly to those who walk closely with Him. The prophet must cultivate an intimate, daily friendship with God. Clarity grows from closeness.

Relationship produces:

- spiritual familiarity
- sensitivity to God's tone
- awareness of God's movement
- recognition of God's patterns
- trust in God's character

The prophet hears God fluently because they spend time with Him consistently. Listening becomes natural when the heart is connected, surrendered, and attentive.

2. GOD SPEAKS IN MULTIPLE WAYS—AND THE PROPHET MUST LEARN THEM ALL

God is not limited to a single method of communication. Just as a parent uses different tones and methods depending on the situation, God speaks through diverse channels. The prepared prophet must learn to recognize His voice in many forms.

God speaks through Scripture.
The Bible is the clearest, most authoritative form of divine communication. Every prophetic revelation must align with Scripture's truth.

God speaks through the inner whisper of the Spirit.
This is the quiet, often subtle voice that speaks to the heart.

God speaks through impressions and internal nudges.
These are gentle pushes or pulls in the spirit that alert the prophet to something important.

God speaks through dreams.
Dreams may be symbolic or literal but often carry prophetic insight.

God speaks through visions.
These may come in images, scenes, or spiritual flashes that communicate revelation.

God speaks through peace or unrest.
Peace may confirm God's will, while unrest warns the prophet to pause.

God speaks through circumstances.
Doors open or close in alignment with His guidance.

God speaks through other believers.

Another prophetic voice may confirm what God has already spoken.

God occasionally uses audible signs, inner knowing, or angelic visitation.

The prophet must not limit God. The more they learn His ways, the clearer His voice becomes.

3. THE PROPHET MUST QUIET INTERNAL NOISE

Hearing God clearly requires internal stillness. Many believers struggle not because God is silent but because their minds are noisy.

Internal noise includes:

- anxiety
- overthinking
- personal ambition
- emotional turbulence
- fear
- inner conflict
- frustration
- exhaustion
- past trauma
- unhealed wounds

When the soul is loud, the Spirit's whisper is drowned out. The prepared prophet intentionally cultivates inner silence. They practice stillness, meditation on Scripture, deep worship, and reflective prayer to quiet the heart.

Clear hearing requires a quiet spirit.

4. DISCERNMENT IS THE PROPHET'S FILTER

Discernment is the ability to distinguish the voice of God from:

- the voice of self,
- the voice of emotion,
- the voice of culture,
- the voice of people,
- and the voice of the enemy.

Discernment comes through:

- time with God,
- Scripture study,
- inner healing,
- wise counsel,
- and spiritual maturity.

Without discernment, the prophet may mistake:

- enthusiasm for revelation,
- fear for warning,
- imagination for vision,
- insecurity for conviction,
- or anxiety for divine urgency.

Discernment filters out false signals so that the prophet can hear God accurately.

5. THE ENEMY ALSO SPEAKS—AND THE PROPHET MUST NOT CONFUSE HIS VOICE WITH GOD'S

One of the most dangerous mistakes any prophet can make is to attribute demonic influence to God. The enemy mimics, distorts, distracts, and deceives. He speaks through:

- condemnation,
- confusion,
- accusation,
- manipulation,
- fear,
- intrusive thoughts,
- and emotional instability.

The voice of the enemy always contradicts Scripture, undermines identity, disturbs peace, or pulls the heart away from intimacy. Once the prophet becomes familiar with God's voice, the enemy's lies become easier to identify.

God's voice always produces clarity, conviction, peace, guidance, comfort, or holiness.

The enemy's voice produces fear, shame, confusion, or hopelessness.

6. THE PROPHET MUST GUARD AGAINST WISHFUL HEARING

Wishful hearing happens when a prophet's desires override their discernment. Instead of listening purely, they hear what they want to hear. This can happen when the prophet:

- desires a certain outcome,
- fears a difficult truth,
- is emotionally attached to someone or something,

- or hopes for quick fulfillment.

Wishful hearing distorts revelation. The prepared prophet must separate:

what they hope for from what God has spoken.

They must be willing to hear God even when He challenges their plans, opinions, or comfort.

7. THE PROPHET MUST RESIST THE PRESSURE TO PRODUCE REVELATION

Sometimes prophets feel pressured to hear something profound—especially when others expect them to speak. This pressure can cause them to manufacture revelation rather than wait on God.

The prepared prophet must learn to say:

- "I don't have anything from the Lord right now."
- "Let me pray about it first."
- "I cannot speak without clarity."

Revelation is received, not forced. God speaks to yielded vessels, not pressured minds.

8. HEARING GOD REQUIRES PURITY OF HEART

Purity is essential for prophetic clarity. When sin, bitterness, jealousy, or unforgiveness are present, revelation becomes foggy. A polluted heart produces polluted hearing.

Purity protects the prophetic gift by:

- keeping motives clean,
- ensuring the prophet desires God above all,
- removing internal static,
- and preventing emotional interference.

Purity keeps the prophet aligned with the Spirit, enabling clear hearing.

9. THE PROPHET MUST LISTEN LONGER THAN THEY SPEAK

Many believers rush prayer. They speak quickly, list their needs, and rise without listening. But prophets must cultivate long listening. Listening prayer is where clarity is born.

Listening includes:

- waiting quietly,
- inviting the Spirit to speak,
- lingering in stillness,
- training the heart to perceive,
- and resisting the urge to rush revelation.

God often speaks after the noise of the mind settles. This requires patience.

The prepared prophet becomes an expert listener.

10. GOD'S VOICE ALWAYS ALIGNS WITH HIS CHARACTER

A prophet who knows the heart of God can easily identify His voice. God's voice reflects:

- kindness,
- truth,
- love,
- purity,
- justice,
- compassion,
- patience,
- and holiness.

If a revelation contradicts God's nature, it is not from Him. The prophet must measure every impression against the character of Christ.

God does not speak in ways inconsistent with who He is.

11. CLARITY COMES THROUGH REPETITION AND CONFIRMATION

God often repeats Himself when He wants to strengthen clarity Repetition is not redundancy—it is reinforcement. Confirmation may come through:

- multiple impressions,
- Scripture,
- dreams,
- sermons,
- unexpected conversations,
- or internal peace.

The prepared prophet pays attention to patterns, themes, and repeated messages. God confirms what He wants emphasized.

12. PROPHETS MUST LEARN THE LANGUAGE OF SYMBOLISM

God frequently speaks through symbolic dreams, visions, and impressions. Symbols are not random—they carry prophetic language that must be interpreted spiritually.

For example:

- Water may represent the Spirit or cleansing.
- Fire may represent purification or passion.
- Rooms may represent areas of the soul.
- Keys may represent authority.
- Roads may represent direction.
- Storms may represent warfare or transition.

Prophets must learn God's symbolic vocabulary—not through guesswork, but through prayer, Scripture, and experience.

13. HEARING GOD REQUIRES FILTERING OUT EXTERNAL VOICES

The prophet lives in a world saturated with voices—news, social media, culture, entertainment, opinions, commentary, and noise. To hear God clearly, the prophet must intentionally limit these influences.

Too many external voices create:

- distraction,
- confusion,
- comparison,
- emotional overload,
- and spiritual dullness.

The prepared prophet practices seasons of digital fasting, mental rest, and disciplined focus. They create space for God by reducing noise.

14. CLARITY STRENGTHENS WHEN THE PROPHET OBEYS QUICKLY

Obedience sharpens spiritual hearing. When a prophet obeys God promptly, their sensitivity increases. When they delay or resist, their sensitivity weakens.

Obedience opens spiritual hearing like a door. Disobedience closes it.

The prophet must guard sensitivity by living obediently, even when obedience is inconvenient.

15. PROPHETS MUST TEST THEIR HEARING THROUGH ACCOUNTABILITY

Even seasoned prophets must test what they hear by submitting revelation to:

- pastors,
- mentors,
- wise believers,
- and Scripture.

Accountability protects the prophet from misinterpretation. It ensures that revelation is processed with humility, wisdom, and community. Testing prophetic hearing is not doubt—it is maturity.

A prophet who cannot be checked cannot be trusted.

CONCLUSION: THE SHEPHERD'S VOICE IS CLEAR TO THE HEART THAT IS QUIET, PURE, AND SURRENDERED

Hearing God clearly is not about dramatic encounters—it is about relational closeness, spiritual discipline, purity of heart, and consistent listening. The prepared prophet does not panic when God seems quiet nor rush when He seems delayed. They walk with Him daily, cultivating spiritual sensitivity until His voice becomes unmistakable.

This is the call of the prepared prophet—
to hear God in a world of noise,
to discern His whisper among competing voices,
to recognize His direction in the midst of confusion,
and to follow His leading with unwavering faith.

The prophet who hears God clearly becomes a vessel of accuracy, wisdom, humility, and power.

14

⟨✤⟩

Prophetic Vision and Foresight

Seeing Beyond the Natural Into God's Future Plans

INTRODUCTION: THE PROPHET SEES WHAT OTHERS DO NOT SEE

Prophets are not merely hearers of God's voice—they are seers of God's perspective. They see beyond the surface, beyond the moment, and beyond the visible. They observe life not just horizontally, but vertically, through the lens of Heaven. Prophetic vision is not imagination; it is divine insight. It is God enabling a prophet to perceive spiritual realities, upcoming seasons, hidden truths, and future outcomes long before they manifest in the natural world.

Prophetic foresight is not fortune-telling. It is not prediction. It is revelation born from intimacy, discernment, and the Spirit's illumination. It is God allowing a prophet to glimpse His plans, purposes, warnings, promises, and direction so they can align, intercede, and prepare.

This chapter explores how the prepared prophet develops prophetic vision, interprets it with wisdom, and uses foresight to strengthen the Body of Christ.

1. PROPHETIC VISION BEGINS WITH GOD'S PERSPECTIVE, NOT HUMAN INTERPRETATION

Before a prophet can see spiritually, they must learn to see differently. Natural sight is limited. It is shaped by circumstances, past experiences, fears, emotions, and assumptions. But prophetic vision requires the prophet to surrender their personal lens and adopt God's perspective.

Seeing as God sees means:

- looking at situations through faith,
- recognizing spiritual activity behind natural events,
- understanding divine purpose in suffering or delay,
- perceiving potential in people others dismiss,
- and viewing the future through promise rather than fear.

Prophetic vision is not about predicting events—it is about perceiving God's intention.

2. PROPHETS ARE SEERS BECAUSE THEY ARE WATCHERS

Prophets see clearly because they watch intentionally. They do not casually observe life—they study it with spiritual sensitivity. Prophets notice emotional shifts, spiritual atmospheres, behavioral patterns, and divine timing. They remain spiritually alert when others relax into comfort.

Watching includes:

- watching in prayer,
- watching in worship,
- watching in Scripture,
- watching in spiritual environments,
- watching over the church,
- watching over families and regions,
- watching for the movement of the Spirit.

Prophetic vision sharpens when the prophet becomes a watcher, alert and attentive to the unseen.

3. GOD OFTEN REVEALS THE FUTURE IN SEED FORM

Prophetic foresight rarely comes as a completed picture. Instead, it often begins as:

- a flash of insight,
- a symbolic dream,
- a faint impression,
- a Scripture that stands out with unusual force,
- a vision with spiritual imagery,
- or a sense of what is coming without full clarity.

The prepared prophet must learn that small impressions can carry great significance. God reveals in seed form because He invites the prophet into relationship, interpretation, and maturity.

Seed-sized revelation requires:

- patience,
- discernment,
- prayer,
- humility,
- processing,
- and gradual unfolding.

Prophets grow as they steward small insights faithfully.

4. PROPHETIC VISION REQUIRES PURITY OF IMAGINATION

Prophets often receive revelation in symbolic form through dreams, visions, and inner imagery. For this imagery to remain accurate, the prophet's imagination must be pure, grounded, and surrendered.

The imagination becomes prophetic when:

- it is controlled by Scripture,
- guided by the Spirit,
- cleansed of impurity,
- disciplined through prayer,
- and humbled before God's wisdom.

A prophet with an undisciplined imagination will confuse inner fantasy with divine vision. But when imagination is purified, it becomes a canvas for prophetic revelation.

5. PROPHETIC FORESIGHT IS NOT ALWAYS PREDICTIVE—SOMETIMES IT IS PREVENTATIVE

Many assume that prophecy always reveals what will happen, but often it reveals what could happen if the people of God do not align with His will. Some visions come to warn. Others come to guide. Some come to prevent disaster. Others come to redirect.

A prophecy of warning is not a prediction of doom—it is an invitation to intercession.

The prepared prophet discerns:

- whether a vision shows God's intention,
- whether it shows a possible outcome,
- or whether it reveals a danger that prayer can prevent.

Prophetic foresight reveals the future so it can be shaped, not merely observed.

6. PROPHETS MUST DISCERN THE TIMING OF THE VISION

Prophetic vision always involves timing—but timing is rarely revealed immediately. Some visions concern:

- the present moment,
- the near future,
- the distant future,
- a person's next season,

- a church's coming assignment,
- a nation's upcoming challenge,
- or a generational shift.

Visions without timing lead to confusion. Prophetic timing requires:

- patience,
- clarity,
- multiple confirmations,
- wisdom from leadership,
- and understanding God's pace.

The prepared prophet learns that timing transforms revelation into guidance.

7. PROPHETIC INSIGHT MUST BE INTERPRETED WITH WISDOM

Vision without interpretation is incomplete. Many prophets receive revelation accurately but interpret it poorly. Interpretation is the skill of understanding:

- what God meant,
- what the symbols represent,
- who the vision is for,
- what action is required,
- and how the word should be applied.

Interpretation requires:

- prayer,
- Scripture,

- discernment,
- humility,
- and often counsel from seasoned mentors.

God speaks in symbolism to deepen the prophet, not confuse them. Interpretation is learned through practice and dependence on the Spirit.

8. PROPHETS MUST DISTINGUISH BETWEEN LITERAL AND SYMBOLIC VISION

Not every prophetic picture is literal. Some visions are metaphors of spiritual truths. The prophet must discern the difference.

For example:

- Seeing a flood may symbolize overwhelming circumstances.
- Seeing a locked door may symbolize delayed opportunity.
- Seeing a bridge may symbolize transition or reconciliation.
- Seeing a wildfire may symbolize revival or purification.
- Seeing chains may symbolize bondage or oppression.
- Seeing a harvest field may symbolize evangelistic opportunity.

Prophets must avoid assuming every detail is literal. Symbolic vision must be interpreted through Scripture and spiritual sensitivity.

9. PROPHETIC VISION REQUIRES EMOTIONAL NEUTRALITY

Emotional attachment can distort prophetic insight. When a prophet wants something to happen—or fears something might happen—they may misread revelation.

The prophet must learn to:

- quiet emotional preferences,
- detach personal desires,
- release fear,
- surrender bias,
- and receive revelation without interference.

A calm spirit produces clear vision.

Prophets must see with God's heart, not their own emotional filter.

10. PROPHETIC VISION OFTEN INCLUDES SEEING POTENTIAL IN PEOPLE

Prophets are uniquely gifted to see beyond a person's present state into their God-given destiny. They see:

- potential beyond brokenness,
- leadership in someone insecure,
- spiritual gifts in someone overlooked,
- purpose in someone wandering,
- and calling in someone unsure of themselves.

Prophetic vision sees people through the lens of redemption. Where others see failure, prophets often see future success. Seeing potential helps prophets:

- encourage,
- awaken calling,
- confirm God's voice,
- and activate spiritual growth.

Prophets build people by helping them see what God sees.

11. PROPHETIC VISION MUST BE ANCHORED IN SCRIPTURE

Scripture is the prophet's compass. All vision must align with the Word. Scripture:

- defines the boundaries of prophetic revelation,
- protects the prophet from deception,
- provides context for interpreting symbols,
- anchors the prophet when visions seem unusual,
- and confirms God's patterns and principles.

Prophetic foresight becomes dangerous when Scripture is not its foundation. The prepared prophet keeps both the Bible and the Spirit at the center of their vision.

12. PROPHETIC VISION MUST BE TESTED AND CONFIRMED

Before releasing a prophetic vision, the prophet must test it. Tests include:

- confirmation through Scripture,
- agreement with God's character,
- alignment with prophetic patterns,
- inner peace,
- counsel from leaders,
- and repeated impressions.

A vision that does not withstand testing is not ready for release. Prophets must avoid rushing to speak before revelation is confirmed.

Confidence increases with confirmation.

13. PROPHETIC VISION MUST NOT PRODUCE FEAR, CONFUSION, OR MANIPULATION

Even when visions are corrective or warning in nature, they must be delivered with love and clarity. Prophetic vision should:

- reveal truth,
- bring direction,
- deepen faith,
- inspire preparation,
- and draw people closer to God.

Visions that create fear, panic, or hopelessness often reflect misinterpretation or emotional interference.

Prophetic insight should bring:

- sobriety,
- not anxiety;
- conviction,
- not condemnation;
- preparation,
- not panic.

The prophet must reflect the heart of God, not the intensity of the moment.

14. PROPHETIC VISION OFTEN REVEALS SEASONS

Prophets frequently see upcoming seasons in a person's life. These seasons may involve:

- change or transition,
- growth or pruning,
- elevation or testing,
- promotion or preparation,
- warfare or breakthrough,
- new relationships or closed doors.

Understanding seasons helps the prophet provide clarity without dictating decisions. Prophets do not control seasons—they reveal them so people can align with God's timeline.

15. VISION MUST ALWAYS LEAD TO ACTION OR ALIGNMENT

Prophetic foresight is never given for information alone. Every vision carries purpose. It invites:

- prayer,
- preparation,
- repentance,
- intercession,
- faith,
- or obedience.

If a vision does not produce change, alignment, or understanding, it may not be interpreted correctly. The prepared prophet asks:

"What does God want us to do with this revelation?"

Prophetic vision is a call to movement, not observation.

CONCLUSION: PROPHETS ARE GUARDIANS OF GOD'S FORESIGHT

Prophetic vision is a sacred gift that allows the prophet to see through Heaven's eyes. It is not a talent—it is responsibility. God entrusts prophets with foresight so they can prepare His people, protect His church, and partner with His purposes.

The prepared prophet sees:

- beyond the moment into the future,
- beyond the natural into the spiritual,
- beyond the visible into the invisible,
- beyond the temporary into the eternal.

They carry God's perspective into the earth, helping others understand what God is doing, what God is saying, and what God is preparing to bring forth.

Prophetic vision is not simply sight—it is stewardship.
It is not simply revelation—it is responsibility.
It is not simply insight—it is invitation to alignment with God.

This is the sight of the prepared prophet—vision sharpened by intimacy, tested by Scripture, interpreted with wisdom, and delivered with humility.

15

Prophetic Warning and Correction

Delivering Hard Truth With Love, Wisdom, and Authority

INTRODUCTION: THE PROPHET'S HARDEST ASSIGNMENT IS OFTEN THE MOST NECESSARY

If encouragement comforts the people of God, and guidance directs them, then prophetic warning protects them. Warning and correction are among the most challenging assignments a prophet must ever carry. These messages often involve confronting sin, addressing spiritual danger, exposing deception, or redirecting God's people when they have drifted from His will.

These assignments are difficult because they demand extraordinary courage, maturity, and emotional stability. They also require enormous love. A prophet who corrects without compassion becomes harsh. A prophet who warns without wisdom becomes reckless. A prophet who confronts without humility becomes spiritually dangerous.

Yet, when done correctly, prophetic warning and correction save lives, restore churches, preserve destinies, protect leaders, and prevent spiritual disaster.

This chapter equips the prepared prophet to deliver difficult truth with integrity, precision, and the heart of God.

1. PROPHETIC WARNING ORIGINATES IN LOVE, NOT ANGER

A prophetic warning is not a spiritual scolding. It is an expression of God's love and protection. God warns because He cares. He corrects because He wants His people to flourish. He confronts sin because sin destroys.

A healthy prophet must check their motives before delivering any corrective word. The heart must be cleansed of:

- frustration,
- personal offense,
- emotional reaction,
- self-righteousness,
- impatience,
- or disappointment.

Prophetic warning must be birthed from compassion, tenderness, and genuine concern for the person's soul. If the prophet does not carry God's heart of love, they are not ready to carry God's word of warning.

2. WARNING AND CORRECTION ARE PART OF THE PROPHETIC ASSIGNMENT

Some prophets enjoy encouraging words but avoid corrective messages. Yet Scripture shows that warning is central to prophetic ministry. Biblical prophets often:

- called nations to repentance,
- confronted kings,
- exposed sin,
- corrected idolatry,
- warned about consequences,
- and guided people back to righteousness.

A prophet is not mature until they can deliver both comfort and correction, both encouragement and exposure, both promise and warning.

Corrective prophecy is not negativity—it is spiritual accountability.

3. CORRECTION MUST ALWAYS ALIGN WITH SCRIPTURE

A prophetic correction must be rooted in Scripture, not personal preference. The prophet is not the moral judge—God is. Warning must call people into alignment with God's written truth.

Correction that contradicts Scripture is false. Correction that exceeds Scripture is abusive. Correction that aligns with Scripture is holy.

The prepared prophet studies the Bible deeply to ensure that their warnings are not emotional opinions but divine truth.

4. THE PROPHET MUST CONFIRM THE WORD BEFORE SPEAKING

Warning is weighty. Because of this weight, the prophet must confirm the word through:

- prayer,
- Scripture,
- repeated impressions,
- inner peace,
- counsel from trusted leaders,
- and submission to spiritual authority when appropriate.

Some warnings are private. Others are public. Some are urgent. Others are preventive. Confirmation clarifies timing, audience, and method.

Premature correction can cause confusion.

Confirmed correction brings transformation.

5. WARNING MUST ALWAYS BE PRIVATE BEFORE IT IS EVER PUBLIC

A prophet should never expose a person publicly unless God explicitly commands it—and such moments are extremely rare. Most prophetic correction should be delivered privately, respectfully, and with honor.

Public correction without necessity becomes humiliation, not ministry.

Private correction builds trust.

Public correction should be exceptional and Spirit-led.

The prepared prophet values dignity.

6. PROPHETS MUST DISTINGUISH BETWEEN SIN, MISTAKE, WEAKNESS, AND PROCESS

Not every issue requires the same level of correction. The prophet must discern whether they are addressing:

- **Sin** — disobedience or rebellion
- **Mistake** — error requiring guidance
- **Weakness** — an area needing discipleship
- **Process** — a stage of spiritual development

Correction becomes harmful when the prophet treats weaknesses as sins or treats a developmental process like rebellion. Discernment determines the tone, urgency, and depth of the warning.

7. THE PROPHET MUST AVOID HARSHNESS AND EMBARRASSMENT

Correction loses effectiveness when it wounds unnecessarily. Harshness closes hearts. Shame silences people. Embarrassment destroys trust.

The prophet must avoid:

- humiliating language,
- aggressive tone,
- accusatory statements ("You always..." "You never..."),
- emotional intensity,
- or a spirit of superiority.

The goal is restoration, not destruction.
The method must reflect Christ, not anger.

8. PROPHETIC CORRECTION MUST BE SPECIFIC, NOT VAGUE

General warnings such as "something is wrong" or "you're off track" without clarity can create confusion, fear, or insecurity. The prophet must be specific enough to bring understanding but wise enough not to overshare.

Effective correction is:

- clear,
- concise,
- direct,
- actionable,
- and guided by Scripture.

Vague warnings breed anxiety. Specific ones bring direction.

9. PROPHETIC CORRECTION MUST ALWAYS INCLUDE A REDEMPTIVE PATH

Warning without hope becomes cruelty. Correction without a path forward becomes condemnation. The prophet must always offer:

- Scripture for healing,
- guidance for repentance,
- encouragement for restoration,
- steps toward alignment,
- and assurance of God's mercy.

God corrects to restore, not to destroy.
The prophet must reflect the Redeemer, not the accuser.

10. PROPHETS MUST DELIVER WARNING WITH EMOTIONAL STABILITY

Corrective prophecy demands emotional composure. The prophet must not:

- cry uncontrollably,
- shout in anger,
- speak with agitation,
- show visible frustration,
- or convey personal disappointment.

Emotion can cloud perception. Correction must come through spiritual calmness. Prophets must be emotionally grounded before delivering difficult truth.

11. TIMING DETERMINES EFFECTIVENESS

A corrective word delivered at the wrong moment loses impact. Timing is a prophetic skill The prophet must ask:

- "Is the person emotionally ready?"
- "Is this the right environment?"
- "Is God saying 'now,' 'later,' 'or 'wait'?"
- "Should I share the full word or only part?"

Warning delivered out of season becomes weight, not guidance. The prepared prophet waits for the Spirit's timing.

12. PROPHETS MUST NEVER USE CORRECTION TO CONTROL PEOPLE

Correction becomes toxic when used to manipulate, dominate, or influence personal decisions. Prophets must avoid:

- telling people whom to marry,
- dictating career choices,
- controlling where people live,
- making decisions for families,
- or using fear to get compliance.

The prophet's role is to reveal God's heart, not replace the Holy Spirit. Manipulative correction is spiritual abuse. True prophetic correction empowers people to choose obedience.

13. PROPHETIC WARNING OFTEN CONFRONTS HIDDEN SIN

Prophets may discern sin that others cannot see. When this happens, the prophet must handle the revelation delicately. The goal is not exposure—it is redemption. The prophet must:

- speak privately,
- show compassion,
- reference Scripture,
- guide the person toward repentance,
- and encourage accountability.

Exposing sin publicly without necessity destroys trust and violates God's heart.

God reveals privately what He desires redeemed privately.

14. PROPHETS MUST CONFRONT FALSE TEACHING AND DECEPTION WISELY

Sometimes correction involves addressing doctrinal error or spiritual deception. In these cases, the prophet must approach with:

- deep biblical grounding,
- calm authority,
- respect,
- patience,
- and clarity.

The goal is not to win debates—it is to guard truth. Corrective prophecy concerning doctrine must always point back to Scripture as the authority.

15. PROPHETIC WARNING MUST BE BALANCED WITH GRACE

Prophets must never forget they are dealing with human hearts. People are fragile. They are growing. They are maturing. Grace must cover every word of correction.

Grace says:

- "You can recover."
- "God has not left you."
- "There is still hope."
- "You are not disqualified."
- "This correction is an invitation, not a rejection."

Grace protects the soul while truth heals the wound.

CONCLUSION: WARNING IS THE PROPHET'S MOST LOVING MINISTRY

Prophetic warning and correction are not harsh assignments—they are expressions of divine love. The prepared prophet understands that God uses warnings to protect His people, preserve destinies, and prevent destruction. A warning given in love can save a marriage, rescue a ministry, redirect a life, expose deception, stop sin, and restore identity.

Correction is not the prophet's weapon—it is God's invitation for people to return to His heart.

When the prophet delivers warning with:

- humility,
- love,
- clarity,
- wisdom,
- compassion,
- Scripture,
- and timing,

...the result is transformation, healing, and breakthrough.

This is the heart of the prepared prophet—
a vessel willing to speak truth even when it is hard,
to correct with tenderness even when the message is strong,
and to warn with courage even when the audience resists.

A prophet who can deliver correction well is a prophet God can trust deeply.

16

⟨⟩⟨⟩⟨⟩

Walking With God Like Enoch

The Path of Unbroken Intimacy and Heavenly Agreement

INTRODUCTION: WHEN GOD BECOMES THE PROPHET'S DAILY COMPANION

There are prophets who hear God.
There are prophets who serve God.
There are prophets who obey God.

But Enoch was a prophet who walked with God.

Enoch represents the highest calling of prophetic life—not public ministry, not prophetic accuracy, not miraculous encounters, but unbroken communion. Enoch is the portrait of a prophet who lived in such closeness with God that Heaven became more familiar to him than earth. He lived in such alignment that God simply transitioned him from time into eternity without seeing death.

Enoch did not walk with God occasionally.
He walked with God continually.

He did not seek God for words.
He sought God for fellowship.

He did not visit God's presence.
He lived in it.

This chapter equips the prophet to cultivate Enoch's lifestyle—walking with God in depth, purity, sensitivity, and closeness so profound that the boundary between Heaven and earth becomes thin.

1. THE MYSTERY OF ENOCH'S WALK: A LIFE OF CONTINUOUS AGREEMENT

Scripture describes Enoch's life in one breathtaking sentence: "Enoch walked with God."

Walking implies:

- movement,
- consistency,
- direction,
- alignment,
- partnership,
- and relational rhythm.

Prophetic ministry is not a sprint of revelation—it is a walk. Not a moment of visitation—a lifestyle of habitation. Enoch learned to agree with God in such sustained intimacy that his life became a prophetic statement.

To walk with God means:

- to want what God wants,
- to love what God loves,
- to resist what God resists,
- to stay where God stays,
- to move when God moves,
- to feel what God feels,
- to think what God thinks.

The prepared prophet must understand:
Walking with God is not an event. It is identity.

2. ENOCH WALKED WITH GOD IN A WICKED GENERATION—SO MUST THE PROPHET

Enoch's world was morally collapsing. Violence, corruption, and spiritual rebellion filled the earth. Yet Enoch maintained an unbroken walk with God in the midst of cultural darkness.

This shows that intimacy with God is not dependent on environment—it is dependent on consecration.

Prophets today live in a world of:

- spiritual distractions,
- moral compromise,
- cultural pressure.

- counterfeit spirituality,
- and technological noise.

Yet the prophet called to walk like Enoch must learn to build intimacy in the middle of noise, purity in a world of impurity, and devotion in a world of spiritual apathy.

The darker the environment, the more radiant the walk.

3. THE ENOCH WALK BEGINS WITH HUNGER, NOT SKILL

Prophets often develop skills—discernment, interpretation, delivery, timing—but the Enoch dimension is not attained through gifting. It is birthed through hunger.

Hunger says:

- "I must know You."
- "I desire Your nearness more than ministry."
- "I want Your presence more than Your power."
- "I crave Your heart more than Your hand."
- "Nothing satisfies me except You."

Without hunger, the prophet becomes a performer.
With hunger, the prophet becomes a companion of God.

Enoch did not walk with God because he was a prophet.
He walked with God because he was hungry.

4. THE PROPHET MUST BUILD A LIFE GOD ENJOYS

Many believers want to enjoy God, but few consider whether God enjoys them. Enoch lived a life so pleasing to God that Heaven longed for his company.

A life God enjoys is marked by:

- humility,
- holiness,
- obedience,
- surrender,
- compassion,
- faith,
- and purity.

The goal is not to impress God but to please Him. The prepared prophet must examine their habits, conversations, silence, responses, and inner thoughts and ask:

"Does this attract God or repel Him?"

When God enjoys a prophet's life, He draws near effortlessly.

5. WALKING WITH GOD REQUIRES INTERNAL STILLNESS

Enoch developed quietness of soul. Without inner stillness, intimacy is impossible. The prophet must silence:

- fear,
- anxiety,
- ambition,
- impatience,

- busyness,
- emotional noise,
- and internal chatter.

Stillness creates space for God's whisper.
Noise suffocates nearness.

The prophet must become deeply comfortable with silence—not empty silence, but sacred, expectant, peaceful silence where God's presence becomes tangible.

6. ENOCH WALKED IN SUCH AGREEMENT THAT HE BECAME A PROPHETIC PORTAL

Enoch was not merely a man who prayed. He became a man through whom God could express Himself. His walk created a spiritual gateway for revelation.

Prophets who walk like Enoch become:

- carriers of divine presence,
- interpreters of Heaven's rhythm,
- voices of divine perspective,
- atmospheres of holiness,
- conduits of God's movement.

Their very presence shifts environments.
Their steps create spiritual openings.
Their words carry weight because their walk carries God.

A prophet who walks deeply with God becomes a portal—not of ego, but of eternity.

7. WALKING WITH GOD INVITES HEAVENLY ENCOUNTERS

Enoch's walk gave him access to realms beyond human understanding. His intimacy opened visionary dimensions. Prophets who walk like Enoch often experience:

- supernatural dreams,
- angelic activity,
- revelatory visions,
- divine counsel,
- spiritual transport in prayer,
- encounters with God's glory,
- and prophetic downloads that shape generations.

These encounters are not sought—they emerge naturally out of proximity.

Where intimacy increases, revelation intensifies.

8. ENOCH WALKED WITH GOD UNTIL EARTH COULD NO LONGER HOLD HIM

Enoch did not suddenly vanish—he gradually transitioned. With each year of intimacy, he became less attached to earth and more attuned to eternity. Eventually, the distance between Heaven and earth shrank until translation became the next natural step.

For prophets today, walking like Enoch produces:

- detachment from worldly values,
- loosening of material desires,
- deeper longing for spiritual truth,
- increased sensitivity to Heaven,
- an eternal mindset,

- and a life oriented toward God's heart.

The prophet who walks closely with God may live on earth but is not bound by it.
They live with Heaven in their eyes.

9. THE ENOCH WALK REQUIRES RADICAL OBEDIENCE

Walking with God means agreeing with His direction even when it contradicts:

- personal comfort,
- human expectations,
- cultural norms,
- religious traditions,
- emotional preference,
- or logical understanding.

Obedience is not a burden—it is the prophet's joy. Obedience is not restriction—it is alignment. Obedience is not punishment—it is positioning.

Enoch did not negotiate with God.
He yielded to God.

Prophets today must rediscover radical obedience if they want Enoch-level intimacy.

10. ENOCH WALKED CONSISTENTLY, NOT OCCASIONALLY

Many walk with God during:

- crisis,
- spiritual inspiration,
- emotional highs,
- or supernatural experiences.

But the Enoch walk is daily.
Ordinary.
Uninterrupted.
Steady.

It is not built on moods but habits.
Not on feelings but faithfulness.

The prophet must develop spiritual rhythms:

- daily prayer without hurry,
- Scripture reading without agenda,
- worship without performance,
- stillness without distraction,
- listening without impatience,
- obedience without delay.

Consistency builds intimacy.
Intimacy builds revelation.

11. WALKING WITH GOD MAKES THE PROPHET A FRIEND OF HEAVEN

There is a difference between servants, children, and friends:

- A servant obeys commands.
- A child enjoys benefits.
- A friend knows secrets.

Enoch entered the friend dimension.
Friends gain access to God's confidential counsel.

Prophets who walk deeply with God become:

- friends of Heaven,
- confidants of the Spirit,
- keepers of revelation,
- carriers of divine secrets,
- and stewards of God's mysteries.

God does not whisper secrets to distant acquaintances.
He reveals them to close companions.

12. THE ENOCH WALK REQUIRES FEARLESSNESS

Walking closely with God means walking in a direction few understand. Prophets who pursue intimacy experience:

- misunderstanding,
- loneliness,
- critique,
- jealousy,
- and distance from those unwilling to walk deeper.

But closeness with God is worth any cost.
The prophet must fear God more than people.

The Enoch walk is fearless because the prophet is anchored in fellowship, not approval.

13. INTIMACY PROTECTS THE PROPHET FROM DECEPTION

Prophets face constant spiritual voices—divine, human, and demonic. Intimacy becomes the filter. When a prophet walks closely with God:

- deception becomes obvious,
- counterfeit spirits become detectable,
- emotional impulses lose influence,
- spiritual confusion fades,
- and the prophet becomes immune to manipulation.

Deception thrives in distance.
Clarity thrives in closeness.

Walking with God keeps hearing pure.

14. THE ENOCH WALK IS A WALK OF ALIGNMENT, NOT ACHIEVEMENT

Prophetic culture often focuses on:

- gifts,
- platforms,
- accuracy,
- ministry success,
- influence,
- and recognition.

But Enoch pursued none of these.
His life was about alignment—not achievement.

His walk was prophetic because it was relational.

His greatness was intimacy—not performance.

The prepared prophet must remember:
God values closeness more than ministry.
Intimacy precedes influence.
Presence outweighs platform.

15. THE PROPHET MUST LEARN TO "WALK OUT" WHAT GOD REVEALS

Enoch didn't simply receive revelation—he embodied it.
He lived truth.
He walked holiness.
He demonstrated God's heart through his daily life.

Prophets today must not only speak God's word—they must walk God's word.

When the prophet's life becomes revelation, their words become authority.

This is the power of the Enoch walk.

CONCLUSION: WALKING WITH GOD IS THE PROPHET'S HIGHEST CALLING

Enoch shows the prophet the ultimate destination—not a title, not fame, not gifting, not supernatural displays, but unbroken intimacy with God.

To walk with God like Enoch is:

- to breathe Heaven's atmosphere,
- to host God's presence,
- to live in continual agreement,

- to carry divine nearness,
- to embody prophecy,
- to reflect God's heart,
- and to move in step with eternity.

This is the deepest preparation of the prophet—
to walk so closely with God
that earth becomes unfamiliar
and Heaven becomes home.

Enoch walked with God...
and the prepared prophet must do the same.

17

The Weeping Prophet

Carrying God's Burden Like Jeremiah

INTRODUCTION: WHEN THE PROPHET FEELS WHAT GOD FEELS

There is a dimension of prophetic life reserved for those willing to allow God to break their hearts for the sake of His people. It is not glamorous. It is not celebrated. It is not emotionally comfortable. It is costly, painful, and often misunderstood. Yet it is one of the most sacred callings a prophet can walk in.

This dimension is prophetic weeping—the capacity to feel divine grief, sense spiritual danger, and bear emotional burdens on behalf of God's people.

Jeremiah is the clearest biblical example of this calling. He is known as the Weeping Prophet not because he was weak, but because he was spiritually sensitive. His tears were not emotional instability—they were prophetic expression. He cried because God cried. He mourned because Heaven mourned. He lamented because the people refused to listen, and he could feel the consequences before they arrived.

Prophets today must understand that sometimes God calls them to weep—to carry grief, to intercede with tears, to feel spiritual conditions deeply, and to release warning through brokenness rather than anger.

1. PROPHETIC WEEPING IS NOT EMOTIONALISM—IT IS DIVINE EMPATHY

Jeremiah did not weep because he was fragile. He wept because he was connected. His tears flowed from intimacy and empathy with the heart of God. He felt what God felt toward:

- a stubborn nation,
- a rebellious generation,
- a people heading toward judgment,
- priests who lost their passion,
- leaders who misled the nation,
- and a church culture that drifted from truth.

Prophetic weeping is divine empathy—God sharing His heart with the prophet so they can intercede effectively.

This is why prophetic weeping is powerful:
The prophet is not crying alone—God is crying through them.

2. PROPHETS CARRY EMOTIONAL WEIGHT OTHERS CANNOT UNDERSTAND

Jeremiah often felt alone because he carried an emotional and spiritual weight unknown to those around him. Prophetic burden is not always visible. It often manifests as:

- sudden heaviness,
- deep sadness without natural cause,
- tears during prayer,
- a sense of urgency,
- grief over sin,
- or overwhelming compassion for people.

This burden is not depression—it is intercession.
Not anxiety—it is spiritual alertness.
Not weakness—it is divine sensitivity.

Prophets feel the spiritual climate before others do.

3. PROPHETIC TEARS ARE INTERCESSION IN LIQUID FORM

When Jeremiah wept, his tears were prayer. They were intercession without words. Tears express what the mouth cannot articulate. Prophetic tears carry:

- spiritual authority,
- deep intercession,
- divine alignment,
- emotional healing,
- and prophetic breakthrough.

Prophetic tears are not a sign of emotional collapse—they are evidence of spiritual travail.

Some of the prophet's greatest battles are fought through tears, not declarations. Their greatest victories are won through weeping. not shouting.

4. PROPHETS WEEP BECAUSE THEY SEE WHAT OTHERS CHOOSE TO IGNORE

Jeremiah saw the spiritual condition of the people long before they saw it themselves. Prophets today experience the same reality. They often see:

- danger where others see comfort,
- deception where others see entertainment,
- sin where others see culture,
- spiritual decline where others see progress,
- rebellion where others see freedom,
- and drifting where others see normalcy.

Seeing clearly is both a gift and a burden.
The prophet weeps because clarity is heavy.

Prophets do not weep because things are bad.
They weep because they know what will happen if nothing changes.

5. PROPHETS WEEP WHEN PEOPLE REJECT GOD'S WORD

Jeremiah experienced the pain of delivering God's message faithfully only to be:

- ignored,

- mocked,
- rejected,
- persecuted,
- misunderstood,
- and falsely accused.

This pain still exists today.
Prophets feel deep sorrow when people choose:

- sin over sanctification,
- culture over conviction,
- compromise over commitment,
- deception over discernment,
- and rebellion over relationship with God.

Jeremiah did not weep for himself—he wept for the people who resisted God's call.

6. PROPHETIC WEEPING REQUIRES EMOTIONAL MATURITY

The prophet must learn to distinguish between:

- personal emotional pain versus
- divine prophetic burden.

Untrained prophets might confuse the two, leading to emotional instability. But prepared prophets mature in emotional awareness. They learn to ask:

- "Is this God's grief or my own?"
- "Am I weeping from divine burden or personal frustration?"
- "Is this sorrow spiritual or emotional?"

- "Is God inviting me to intercede or simply reflect?"

Emotional maturity allows the prophet to steward tears properly.

7. PROPHETS MUST SUBMIT THEIR TEARS TO GOD

Prophetic weeping must be surrendered, not bottled or dismissed. The prophet must take their tears to God and ask:

- "What do You want me to pray?"
- "What is the meaning of this burden?"
- "What breakthrough are these tears birthing?"
- "Who are these tears for?"
- "What should I speak or not speak?"

Prophetic tears invite revelation when submitted to God.

8. PROPHETS MUST GUARD AGAINST BECOMING BITTER OR RESENTFUL

Jeremiah faced intense loneliness, ridicule, and rejection. Prophets who feel deeply can become vulnerable to:

- disappointment,
- discouragement,
- self-pity,
- resentment,
- and emotional fatigue.

Bitterness will corrupt prophetic clarity.
Resentment will poison the prophet's heart.
Weariness will distort revelation.

The prophet must allow God to heal their emotions regularly. Prophetic tears must remain holy, not wounded.

9. PROPHETIC WEEPING PRODUCES SPIRITUAL BREAKTHROUGH

Jeremiah's weeping shook Heaven. His tears were not wasted—they broke spiritual ground, purified the atmosphere, and opened the way for God's mercy. Prophets today must believe that tears carry power. Weeping:

- breaks spiritual resistance,
- washes away spiritual blindness,
- prepares the soil of hearts,
- softens stubbornness,
- dismantles demonic barriers,
- and ushers in revival.

Tears plow the ground for the seed of the prophetic word.

10. PROPHETS WEEP BECAUSE THEY CARRY GOD'S DESIRE FOR RESTORATION

Jeremiah's tears were not hopeless—they were redemptive. He wept because he desired restoration. He longed for repentance, reconciliation, and spiritual renewal.

This is the difference between prophetic weeping and emotional collapse:

Prophetic tears point toward healing.
Emotional tears stay stuck in pain.

A Jeremiah-level prophet weeps with:

- hope,
- expectation,
- faith,
- compassion,
- and redemptive purpose.

They do not cry as victims—they cry as intercessors.

11. GOD TRUSTS PROPHETS WHO CAN CARRY HIS BURDEN

Not everyone can handle God's emotional weight. It is sacred. It is intense. It requires maturity. Prophets who can weep like Jeremiah carry a deeper level of divine trust.

God entrusts this dimension to prophets who:

- walk in holiness,
- pursue intimacy,
- are emotionally stable,
- remain humble,
- and prioritize God's heart over personal comfort.

Prophets who can cry with God can also prophesy with God.

12. PROPHETIC WEEPING MUST NOT BECOME PROPHETIC DEPRESSION

There is a difference between:

Holy sorrow and hopeless sorrow.
Divine burden and emotional collapse.
God's grief and personal anguish.

The prophet must avoid sinking into despair. Jeremiah struggled with moments of deep sorrow, yet he always returned to God's presence, allowing God to restore his soul.

Prepared prophets must:

- stay anchored in hope,
- stay connected to healthy relationships,
- stay rooted in Scripture,
- and stay poured out before the Lord.

Prophetic burden should drive the prophet to intercession, not isolation.

13. PROPHETIC TEARS MAY PRECEDE PROPHETIC BREAKTHROUGH

Often the prophet will weep before revival hits. They will sense what God is about to do before others perceive it. Tears may come before:

- spiritual awakening,
- deliverance,
- national shifts,
- church revival,
- family restoration,
- or personal transformation.

God invites the prophet to labor emotionally for breakthroughs others will enjoy.

This is prophetic travail—it is birthing through tears.

14. PROPHETS MUST LEARN TO RELEASE THE BURDEN AFTER THE TEARS

The prophet must not carry what God does not ask them to carry After weeping, they must let God lift the burden. Holding onto grief beyond its assignment becomes damaging.

Jeremiah released his burden back to God repeatedly. He poured out his anguish, then rested in God's presence.

Prophets deepen spiritually when they learn:

- to feel deeply,
- to weep fully,
- to pray thoroughly,
- and then to release completely.

15. PROPHETIC WEEPING IS A SIGN OF DEEP LOVE FOR GOD AND HIS PEOPLE

Jeremiah loved God intensely. He also loved people intensely. Prophetic weeping flows from that dual love. Prophets who weep are those:

- who care genuinely,
- who intercede passionately,
- who see clearly,
- who discern spiritually,
- who feel deeply,

- and who carry God's heart faithfully.

Weeping is not weakness.
It is spiritual strength expressed through tenderness.

Jeremiah's tears were his true anointing.

CONCLUSION: PROPHETS WHO WEEP CARRY GOD'S HEART IN THEIR TEARS

To weep like Jeremiah is to enter a sacred dimension of prophetic calling. It is to feel God's pain over sin, His grief over rebellion, His longing for restoration, and His compassion for the broken. Prophetic tears are spiritual keys. They unlock repentance, clear atmospheres, break strongholds, and move Heaven.

The prepared prophet must learn that:

God does not only speak through their mouth—
sometimes He speaks through their tears.

There will be seasons when words fail but tears speak.
There will be moments when weeping becomes warfare.
There will be burdens that can only be carried through tears.

Jeremiah's example teaches the prophet that deep sensitivity is not a liability—it is a calling.
And the prophet who embraces this sacred burden walks in profound partnership with the heart of God.

18

The Crushing of the Prophet

Refinement, Isolation, and the Making of a Pure Vessel

INTRODUCTION: BEFORE GOD TRUSTS A PROPHET PUBLICLY, HE BREAKS THEM PRIVATELY

Every authentic prophet walks through seasons of crushing—seasons where God strips away the unnecessary, confronts the flesh, refines motives, and purifies calling. Crushing is not punishment; it is preparation. It is not God's rejection; it is His investment. It is the divine sculpting that transforms a gifted individual into a trustworthy vessel.

The crushing is painful, yet it is holy. It is uncomfortable, yet it is purposeful. It is lonely, yet it is sacred. Without crushing, a prophet becomes shallow. Without breaking, a prophet becomes dangerous.

Without refinement, a prophet becomes prideful, impulsive, or emotionally unstable.

God crushes the prophet not to destroy them, but to ensure that nothing within them can destroy their calling.

1. CRUSHING IS GOD'S METHOD OF REMOVING SELF-RELIANCE

The prophetic gift is powerful, and with power comes the temptation of self-sufficiency. If God allowed prophets to operate fully in their gift without breaking their self-reliance, they would eventually trust in:

- their ability to hear,
- their ability to discern,
- their ability to minister,
- their ability to interpret dreams,
- their influence,
- or their reputation.

Crushing dismantles the illusion of independence. Through hardship, the prophet learns:

- to lean fully on God,
- to distrust their flesh,
- to surrender their own wisdom,
- and to rely solely on the Spirit.

Prophetic strength is born from prophetic dependence.

2. CRUSHING STRIPS THE PROPHET OF PRIDE

Great revelation can produce great pride if left unchecked. Pride is the most dangerous enemy of prophetic ministry. It blinds. It deceives. It isolates. It corrupts. Therefore, God uses crushing to ensure pride has no place in the prophet's heart.

When God breaks pride, He often allows:

- humbling circumstances,
- unexpected disappointments,
- corrections from leadership,
- seasons of hiddenness,
- and moments where the prophet feels overlooked.

These experiences are not designed to shame the prophet—they are designed to shape them. Pride must die so purity can survive.

3. CRUSHING PURIFIES MOTIVES

Prophets must operate from pure motives. If their motives become polluted with:

- the desire for validation,
- the need for applause,
- the longing for influence,
- the hunger for affirmation,
- or the fear of rejection,

...their words lose weight and their ministry becomes compromised.

Crushing exposes motives. It brings impurities to the surface. It reveals what is hidden beneath good intentions. God allows pressure so the prophet can see themselves clearly. Purity is impossible without exposure.

4. CRUSHING PRODUCES COMPASSION

The most effective prophets are compassionate prophets. But compassion cannot be taught in theory—it must be born in pain. Prophets grow tender when they:

- experience rejection,
- walk through loneliness,
- encounter misunderstanding,
- face financial hardship,
- endure spiritual warfare,
- or wrestle with inner battles.

These experiences soften the prophet's heart. They break harshness. They dismantle judgment. They produce empathy. Prophets who have suffered deeply minister deeply.

Pain becomes a prophetic tutor.

5. CRUSHING DEEPENS THE PROPHET'S PRAYER LIFE

Nothing intensifies prayer like crushing. When the prophet has no strength left, they turn to God in desperation. Desperate prayer becomes:

- raw,
- honest,
- ransformative,
- and intimate.

The prophet learns prayer not as a discipline alone, but as survival. Crushing removes shallow prayer and replaces it with deep communion. It teaches the prophet to:

- cry out to God,
- listen deeply,
- wrestle in the Spirit,
- travail until breakthrough,
- and abide in God's presence.

Crushing produces intercessors.
Intercessors produce breakthrough.

6. CRUSHING IS OFTEN ACCOMPANIED BY ISOLATION

Isolation is one of the most difficult aspects of prophetic formation. Many prophets walk through seasons where:

- friends drift away,
- mentors seem distant,
- family members misunderstand their calling,
- doors close unexpectedly,
- community feels thin,
- and emotional loneliness intensifies.

This isolation is not abandonment—it is divine positioning. God separates prophets so He can shape them privately. Isolation creates space for:

- clarity,
- healing,
- deep reflection,

- spiritual stripping,
- and transformation.

Isolation is not the absence of people.
It is the presence of God without distraction.

7. CRUSHING CONFRONTS HIDDEN IDOLS

Every prophet must face internal idols—things or desires that compete for God's place. Idols may include:

- relationships,
- ministry success,
- ambition,
- reputation,
- spiritual gifts,
- security,
- or comfort.

God uses crushing to expose and dismantle these idols. The prophet must learn to say:

"Lord, You are enough.
If everything else is removed, You are still my portion."

When idols fall, the prophet becomes free.

8. CRUSHING CREATES DISCERNMENT THAT CANNOT BE TAUGHT

Prophets who have walked through breaking seasons develop discernment born from experience. They gain:

- insight into human behavior,
- sensitivity to deception,
- understanding of spiritual warfare,
- recognition of false motives,
- clarity about people's pain,
- and wisdom in ministry dynamics.

Discernment is not learned from books alone.
It is learned through suffering.

Broken prophets see what unbroken prophets overlook.

9. CRUSHING DEVELOPS CHARACTER STRONGER THAN GIFT

Many admire prophetic gifting, but God prioritizes prophetic character. Crushing produces:

- humility,
- patience,
- emotional stability,
- purity,
- gentleness,
- obedience,
- and endurance.

Gift may impress people.
Character pleases God.

Gift may open doors.
Character keeps them open.

Gift may attract crowds.

Character attracts God.

Crushing ensures character grows deeper than gifting.

10. CRUSHING PREPARES THE PROPHET TO CARRY WEIGHTY REVELATION

God cannot entrust heavy revelation to prophets who have fragile character. Some prophetic burdens require:

- stability,
- emotional resilience,
- spiritual maturity,
- wisdom,
- and obedience.

Without crushing, the prophet would mishandle revelation, or collapse under its weight. Crushing strengthens the prophet to carry:

- national warnings,
- generational assignments,
- church correction,
- long-term intercession,
- and spiritual battles.

Crushing enlarges capacity.

11. CRUSHING BREAKS EMOTIONAL IMPULSIVENESS

Prophets often feel deeply. Without crushing, emotional intensity can cause:

- anger,
- frustration,
- impulsive words,
- quick reactions,
- or rash decisions.

Crushing slows the prophet's emotions.
It teaches restraint.
It produces emotional intelligence.

The prophet becomes:

- calmer,
- wiser,
- more stable,
- less reactive,
- more patient.

They speak with authority because their emotions are sanctified.

12. CRUSHING TEACHES THE PROPHET HOW TO SUFFER WITH GOD, NOT APART FROM HIM

The prophet learns that God does not prevent suffering—He accompanies them through it. Crushing teaches the prophet:

- to find God in pain,
- to hear God in silence,
- to trust God in uncertainty,
- to cling to God in darkness,
- to walk with God through loss.

Prophets do not survive crushing by strength—they survive by surrender.

13. CRUSHING REVEALS WHO THE PROPHET IS WITHOUT THE PLATFORM

Prophetic identity must not be tied to ministry activity. Crushing often removes:

- opportunities,
- platforms,
- assignments,
- visibility,
- and spiritual activity.

This forces the prophet to ask:
"Who am I when no one sees me?"

Crushing reveals whether identity is rooted in God or in ministry. The prepared prophet emerges with God-centered identity.

14. CRUSHING PRODUCES UNSHAKEABLE FAITH

Faith deepens when everything else is stripped away. Crushing removes:

- crutches,
- false security,
- shallow beliefs,
- immature faith.

Through crushing, the prophet develops:

- endurance,
- spiritual stability.
- courage,
- perseverance,
- and confidence in God.

Faith forged in fire cannot be shaken by storms.

15. CRUSHING IS TEMPORARY, BUT ITS TRANSFORMATION IS PERMANENT

Crushing seasons feel long, but they are temporary.
Transformation lasts a lifetime.

The prophet emerges:

- purified,
- wiser,
- humbler,
- stronger,
- more discerning,
- and deeply rooted in God.

The crushing is not the end—it is the shaping that releases the next dimension of calling.

The prophet who survives crushing becomes a vessel God can trust with great revelation, great authority, and great responsibility.

CONCLUSION: CRUSHING IS THE FURNACE OF THE PREPARED PROPHET

Crushing is not God's punishment.
It is God's wisdom.

He crushes prophets so their:

- motives may be pure,
- hearts may be tender,
- faith may be strong,
- discernment may be sharp,
- pride may be broken,
- emotions may be stable,
- identity may be secure,
- and character may be deep.

Crushing prepares the prophet for divine assignment. It teaches them to depend on God, to trust His process, and to love Him more deeply than the gift He gave them.

Crushing shapes the prophet into a vessel of honor—a prophet whose voice is not merely powerful but pure; not merely accurate but holy; not merely gifted but surrendered.

This is the crushing that makes the prepared prophet.

19

The Endurance of the Prophet

Finishing Well, Holding the Mantle, and Standing Until the Final Assignment

INTRODUCTION: IT IS NOT HOW A PROPHET BEGINS—IT IS HOW THEY FINISH

Many people can begin a prophetic journey with excitement, passion, and zeal. But the true test of prophetic calling is not in the beginning—it is in the endurance. All throughout Scripture, God reveals that the prophetic mantle is not a sprint; it is a marathon. It is a lifelong assignment requiring strength, faithfulness, stability, and unwavering commitment to God's voice.

A prophet may start with fire, but only the prepared prophet finishes with faithfulness.

A prophet may begin with revelation, but only the prepared prophet ends with steadfastness.

A prophet may enter ministry with passion, but only the prepared prophet leaves a legacy of obedience.

Endurance is not glamorous. It does not produce instant results. It demands resilience, consistency, self-control, humility, and a life anchored in God's presence.

This chapter equips the prophet to carry their mantle faithfully for a lifetime, resisting burnout, overcoming spiritual fatigue, and finishing their prophetic assignment well.

1. ENDURANCE IS THE PROPHET'S PROOF OF AUTHENTIC CALLING

Anyone can claim prophetic gifting, but only those truly called endure hardship, pressure, rejection, loneliness, and spiritual warfare without abandoning the assignment. Endurance is the evidence of divine choosing.

The prophet must understand:

- battles will come,
- delays will come,
- seasons of silence will come,
- misunderstanding will come,
- setbacks will come,
- and spiritual warfare will intensify.

But authentic calling is revealed not by how loudly a prophet speaks in the beginning, but by how consistently they stand at the end.

Endurance separates the called from the curious.

2. A PROPHET MUST LEARN TO STAND ALONE WHEN NECESSARY

Although the prophet needs community, accountability, and spiritual covering, there will be seasons where standing alone is unavoidable. Jeremiah stood alone. Elijah stood alone. Ezekiel stood alone. John the Baptist stood alone. Even Jesus walked through seasons where His closest companions deserted Him.

Standing alone teaches the prophet:

- courage,
- resilience,
- inner strength,
- emotional stability,
- dependence on God,
- and clarity of identity.

Standing alone reveals whether the prophet serves God for approval or for obedience.

3. ENDURANCE REQUIRES A PROPHET TO MASTER LONGEVITY OVER INTENSITY

Many prophets burn bright but burn out. They expend enormous energy in short bursts but lack sustained rhythms that ensure long-term health.

Longevity requires:

- daily prayer rather than occasional spiritual surges,

- healthy rest rather than spiritual exhaustion,
- emotional maintenance rather than internal neglect,
- consistent study rather than hurried preparation,
- manageable commitments rather than overextension,
- and disciplined rhythms rather than chaotic passion.

Prophetic brilliance must be balanced with prophetic pacing. Endurance depends on lifestyle, not intensity.

4. PROPHETS MUST RECOGNIZE AND RESIST BURNOUT

Burnout is not a lack of calling—it is a lack of balance. Burnout occurs when:

- the prophet gives more than they receive,
- the prophet feels responsible for everyone's breakthrough,
- the prophet carries burdens without releasing them,
- the prophet neglects rest,
- the prophet ministers while emotionally depleted,
- or the prophet carries assignments God did not ask them to carry.

Burnout distorts discernment, weakens revelation, and damages emotional health. The prepared prophet learns to identify burnout early and returns to the presence of God for renewal.

The prophet's greatest weapon against burnout is restoration, not more activity.

5. ENDURANCE REQUIRES PROPHETIC RESILIENCE

Resilience is the ability to bounce back from hardship without losing spiritual identity. Prophets will encounter:

- betrayal,
- disappointment,
- false accusations,
- ministry wounds,
- unfulfilled expectations,
- and seasons of spiritual dryness.

Resilient prophets do not quit when they are wounded. They return to God. They allow Him to heal them. They get back up. They continue the assignment.

A wounded prophet is not disqualified.
A quitting prophet is.

6. THE PROPHET MUST GUARD THEIR MANTLE WITH VIGILANCE

The prophetic mantle is precious. It must be protected. The prophet must guard:

- their purity,
- their integrity,
- their emotional boundaries,
- their spiritual life,
- their private devotion,
- and their public witness.

The mantle can be lost to:

- pride,
- compromise,
- scandal,
- disobedience,
- nrepented sin,
- or prolonged spiritual neglect.

Guarding the mantle is an act of stewardship.
Endurance requires vigilance.

7. ENDURANCE IS SUSTAINED BY INTIMACY WITH GOD

Prophets who endure are not the strongest—they are the closest. Intimacy fuels longevity. Without closeness to God, the prophet becomes weary, drained, and spiritually malnourished.

Intimacy provides:

- renewed strength,
- clarity in confusion,
- healing after hurt,
- direction when lost,
- peace in storms,
- and joy in obedience.

The prophet who walks closely with God will finish faithfully.

8. PROPHETS MUST UNDERSTAND SEASONS OF SILENCE

One of the most challenging seasons in a prophet's life is when God becomes quiet. Silence is not abandonment—it is divine strategy. In silence, God:

- deepens hunger,
- strengthens faith,
- tests motives,
- grows maturity,
- reveals hidden character,
- and shifts the prophet to deeper dimensions.

Prophets must not misinterpret silence as rejection.
Silence prepares prophets for new revelation.

9. ENDURANCE REQUIRES SPIRITUAL DISCIPLINE

The prophet must consistently practice disciplines such as:

- prayer,
- fasting,
- studying the Word,
- meditation,
- solitude,
- worship,
- and journaling revelation.

These disciplines anchor the prophet in stability.
Without discipline, calling becomes inconsistent.

Spiritual discipline is the backbone of prophetic endurance.

10. ENDURANCE PROTECTS THE PROPHET FROM SPIRITUAL DRIFT

Drift happens slowly. Prophets drift when:

- the secret place is neglected,
- accountability fades,
- personal holiness diminishes,
- spiritual hunger weakens,
- and ministry becomes mechanical.

Drift is dangerous because it is unnoticed until it becomes drastic. Endurance pulls the prophet back into alignment regularly.

he prophet who examines their heart consistently remains on course.

11. PROPHETS MUST LEARN HOW TO RECOVER AFTER FAILURE

Failure does not end a prophetic calling unless the prophet chooses not to recover. Great prophets have experienced moments of failure, yet they returned to God with humility and renewed focus.

Recovery requires:

- repentance,
- humility,
- honesty,
- accountability,
- and renewed discipline.

The prophet who refuses to recover forfeits their future.
The prophet who humbly returns is restored by grace.

Endurance embraces grace.
Grace empowers endurance.

12. ENDURANCE REQUIRES HEALTHY RELATIONSHIPS

Prophets often prefer isolation, but without healthy support, they weaken over time. God provides:

- spiritual mentors,
- trusted friends,
- pastoral oversight,
- intercessors,
- and godly partners.

These relationships help the prophet:

- stay grounded,
- stay balanced,
- avoid extremes,
- maintain emotional health,
- and recover from burdens.

Endurance is strengthened through community.

13. PROPHETS MUST MAINTAIN THE FIRE OF EARLY PASSION

When a prophet first encounters their mantle, the fire is fresh. Over time, life, pressure, and routine can dull passion. The prophet must intentionally maintain early zeal.

This requires:

- revisiting foundational encounters,
- cultivating lifelong wonder,
- protecting spiritual excitement,
- refusing to become cynical,
- and staying grateful for the privilege of prophetic calling.

A cynical prophet loses clarity.
A passionate prophet remains sharp.

14. ENDURANCE PRODUCES GENERATIONAL INFLUENCE

Prophets who endure do not simply impact their generation—they impact future generations. Endurance positions the prophet to:

- mentor younger prophets,
- raise up successors,
- leave written revelation,
- impart wisdom,
- preserve spiritual legacy,
- and shape long-term destiny.

Prophets who finish well become pillars in the kingdom.

15. FINISHING WELL IS THE PROPHET'S FINAL PROPHECY

At the end of life, a prophet's true testimony is not the visions they saw—but the life they lived. A prophet finishes well when they:

- remain faithful to God,

- maintain integrity,
- guard purity,
- protect the mantle,
- love deeply,
- obey consistently,
- and glorify God through endurance.

A finished life is a fulfilled prophecy.

The prepared prophet endures to the end—not by might, not by gifting, not by influence, but by the anchor of intimacy with God.

CONCLUSION: ENDURANCE IS THE CROWN OF THE PREPARED PROPHET

Endurance is the prophet's final test. It proves maturity, purifies motives, and establishes legacy. The prophet who endures becomes:

- a steady voice,
- a pure vessel,
- a faithful messenger,
- a mature intercessor,
- a guardian of truth,
- a pillar in the Body of Christ,
- and a testament to God's sustaining grace.

Prophetic greatness is not measured by the height of revelation, but by the depth of faithfulness.

To endure is to overcome.
To endure is to mature.
To endure is to finish the race God assigned.

This is the endurance of the prepared prophet—

faithful until the final breath,
steadfast in every season,
unshakeable in every trial,
and unwavering in their walk with God.

20

The Christ-Centered Prophet

Guiding Humanity to the Redeemer
Like Isaiah

INTRODUCTION: THE PROPHET'S HIGHEST CALLING IS TO POINT TO CHRIST

Every prophet carries a unique assignment—some warn, some build, some comfort, some intercede, some declare, and some confront. Yet all true prophetic ministry ultimately converges on one central purpose:

To direct humanity to the redemptive power of Jesus Christ.

This is the prophetic ministry of Isaiah.
Isaiah prophesied not merely about events, nations, or judgments—he prophesied Christ. He saw Him more clearly than any Old Testament prophet. He described His birth, His life, His suffering, His crucifixion, His resurrection, and His eternal kingdom.

Isaiah did not simply speak for God—he spoke of God incarnate.

He lifted the eyes of a broken people toward the One who would heal them.

He showed that prophecy without redemption is incomplete.

A prophet may have accuracy, insight, revelation, and authority, but if Christ is not at the center—
the prophetic ministry is incomplete.

This chapter calls the prepared prophet to walk in the Isaiah dimension—
a Christ-centered, redemptive, hope-infused prophetic mantle that leads humanity to Jesus.

1. EVERY AUTHENTIC PROPHETIC MINISTRY MUST BE ANCHORED IN JESUS CHRIST

Prophecy is not primarily about the future—it is about the One who holds the future. A prophet's greatest responsibility is not merely to reveal mysteries but to point people toward the Messiah.

A Christ-centered prophet:

- directs people to salvation, not just information,
- leads people to repentance, not just spiritual experiences,
- exalts Jesus above their own gifting,
- proclaims redemption, not condemnation,
- carries the heart of the Savior, not the pride of the gifted.

Christ is not an accessory to prophetic ministry—He is the foundation, the message, the fulfillment, and the purpose.

Without Christ, prophecy becomes mystical philosophy.

With Christ, prophecy becomes the voice of Heaven calling people home.

2. ISAIAH'S PROPHETIC MINISTRY REVEALS THE REDEMPTIVE HEART OF GOD

Isaiah lived centuries before Jesus walked the earth, yet he saw the Messiah with breathtaking clarity. He described:

- the virgin birth,
- the coming Savior,
- the Suffering Servant,
- the stripes that heal,
- the redemption of nations,
- the restoration of Israel,
- the government upon His shoulders,
- and the eternal kingdom of the Prince of Peace.

Isaiah did not simply predict events—he revealed the heart of God.

The prophet today must carry the same heart:

- a heart that longs for redemption,
- a heart that grieves over sin,
- a heart that desires reconciliation,
- a heart that sees beyond judgment to restoration,
- a heart that invites humanity to encounter the Savior.

Prophetic ministry without the heart of Isaiah becomes harsh, judgmental, and incomplete.

3. THE PROPHET MUST SEE CHRIST AS THE FULFILLMENT OF ALL PROPHECY

Jesus is the center of the prophetic storyline. All prophecy ultimately points to Him. He is:

- the Seed promised in Genesis,
- the Lamb foreshadowed in Exodus,
- the High Priest revealed in Leviticus,
- the Captain of the Lord's Host in Joshua,
- the Kinsman Redeemer in Ruth,
- the Son of David in Samuel,
- the Suffering Servant in Isaiah,
- and the returning King of Revelation.

Every prophetic theme—judgment, mercy, restoration, deliverance, healing, and hope—finds fulfillment in Christ.

To prophesy without pointing toward Christ is to offer direction without destination.

4. *The Prophet Must Reveal the Compassion of Christ*

Isaiah not only revealed Christ's mission—he revealed Christ's heart. He described a Messiah who:

- carries sorrows,
- heals the brokenhearted,
- lifts the oppressed,
- forgives the repentant,
- comforts the weary,
- restores the fallen,
- and brings light to darkness.

This compassion must mark the modern prophet.

A prophet who cannot reveal the compassion of Christ cannot effectively represent Him.

The true prophet does not crush the wounded—they bind their wounds.
They do not shame the broken—they lift them.
They do not condemn sinners—they lead them to the Redeemer.

This is the Isaiah dimension.

5. Prophets Must Proclaim the Message of Salvation

The greatest prophetic message is not a prediction—it is an invitation. Salvation is the highest revelation a prophet can declare. A prophet must consistently:

- call people to Jesus,
- explain the need for redemption,
- reveal the power of the Cross,
- proclaim forgiveness of sins,
- announce spiritual freedom,
- and point toward eternal hope.

Predictions may intrigue people—
but salvation transforms them.

A prophet who never preaches Christ is not fulfilling divine assignment.

6. THE PROPHET MUST LIFT THE SAVIOR HIGHER THAN THEMSELVES

Isaiah did not elevate his gift—he elevated his God.

The prophet today must refuse to build personal kingdoms or spiritual brands. Their ministry must consistently point away from themselves and toward Christ.

A Christ-centered prophet says:

"Behold the Lamb of God"—
not "Behold the prophet."

"Look to the Savior"—
not "Look to my accuracy."

"Turn to Jesus"—
not "Turn to my gifting."

The greatest prophets disappear behind the glory of the One they proclaim.

7. THE PROPHET SHARES IN THE MISSION OF CHRIST: TO SEEK AND SAVE THE LOST

The prophetic mantle is not simply a ministry tool—it is a rescue assignment. If the prophet does not carry a burden for souls, their prophetic walk is misaligned.

A prophet aligned with Christ:

- weeps for the lost,
- prays for salvation,
- speaks with compassion,
- leads with humility,
- and sees every prophetic word as an invitation to redemption.

The prophet must never forget that Heaven rejoices more over one soul saved than over a thousand prophecies spoken.

8. ISAIAH TEACHES THE PROPHET HOW TO SEE BEYOND SIN INTO REDEMPTION

Isaiah saw Israel's sin clearly—
but he saw their redemption more clearly still.

He saw:

- judgment,
- but also restoration.
- sin,
- but also salvation.
- rebellion,
- but also reconciliation.
- darkness,
- but also a great light.

This dual vision must define the prophet:

the ability to confront sin
without forgetting grace,
and the ability to see redemption
even in the most broken lives.

Prophets who only see sin become harsh.
Prophets who only see grace become permissive.
Prophets who see both become like Isaiah.

9. THE PROPHET MUST PRESENT CHRIST AS THE ONLY TRUE HOPE

In a world crowded with spiritual options, philosophies, ideologies, and self-help systems, the prophet must proclaim that Jesus Christ alone is:

- the way,
- the truth,
- the life,
- the door,
- the redeemer,
- the healer,
- the liberator,
- the Savior,
- and the King.

The prophet must not compromise this message.
They must not dilute the gospel.
They must not trade Christ-centered prophecy for human-centered inspiration.

Hope that is not rooted in Christ is false hope.

10. The Prophet Must Help People See Themselves Through Christ's Redemption

Prophets help people recognize:

- their identity in Christ,
- their forgiveness in Christ,
- their healing through Christ,
- their destiny in Christ,
- their authority in Christ,

- and their purpose through Christ's finished work.

Prophetic ministry is not only about revealing what God plans to do—it is about revealing what Christ has already done.

A prophet who directs people to their own potential without pointing them to Christ's power becomes motivational but not transformational.

11. THE PROPHET MUST DECLARE THE KINGDOM OF CHRIST

Isaiah saw a kingdom that would never end.
He saw a throne that would never be shaken.
He saw a King whose government would bring justice and peace.
He saw nations drawn to the light of the Messiah.

The modern prophet must continue this proclamation:

- Christ reigns over all nations,
- His kingdom is unshakeable,
- His rule is eternal,
- and His authority is absolute.

The prophet is not simply a voice crying about spiritual experiences—they are a herald announcing a King.

12. THE PROPHET MUST REFLECT THE CHARACTER OF CHRIST

Prophetic ministry is not only about speaking—it is about embodying.
The prophet must reflect:

246 - TONY MEDLEY

- Christ's humility,
- Christ's love,
- Christ's courage,
- Christ's purity,
- Christ's compassion,
- Christ's authority.

People should see Christ through the prophet's life—not only through their revelation.

Isaiah spoke of the Messiah; the prepared prophet reflects Him.

13. PROPHETS MUST CALL THE CHURCH BACK TO THE CROSS

The cross is not a doctrine—it is the epicenter of prophetic ministry. The prophet must keep the Church anchored to:

- the sacrifice of Christ,
- the blood of Jesus,
- the forgiveness of sins,
- the victory of the resurrection,
- the hope of eternal life.

A prophet who does not preach the cross is preaching a powerless message.

Isaiah pointed forward to the cross.
The prophet today points backward to the cross.
But both have one message:
Redemption through Christ alone.

14. PROPHETIC WORDS MUST CARRY THE TONE OF THE GOSPEL

Even corrective or warning words must reflect:

- the hope of salvation,
- the invitation to repentance,
- the mercy of God,
- and the possibility of restoration.

Prophecy without the gospel becomes condemnation.
Prophecy with the gospel becomes transformation.

The prophet's tone must reflect Christ's redemptive heart.

15. THE PROPHET'S GREATEST PROPHECY IS JESUS HIMSELF

At the end of a prophet's life, the greatest message they ever uttered must be the name Jesus.

The greatest revelation is Christ.
The greatest fulfillment is Christ.
The greatest hope is Christ.
The greatest prophecy is Christ.

Every prophetic word, vision, picture, dream, and impression must ultimately lead people to:

the Savior of the world,
the Lamb of God,
the King of glory,
the Redeemer of humanity—
Jesus Christ.

CONCLUSION: THE CHRIST-CENTERED PROPHET
IS THE TRUE PROPHET

Isaiah did not point people to himself—he pointed them to Jesus. The prophet today must follow the same path:

- directing hearts to the Savior,
- calling people to redemption,
- proclaiming the gospel with boldness,
- revealing the compassion of Christ,
- carrying the heart of the Redeemer,
- and keeping Jesus at the center of every prophetic assignment.

The prepared prophet does not simply guide people into their future—they guide people into eternity.

They do not simply speak about destiny—they speak about the Redeemer who guarantees it.

This is the crown of prophetic ministry—to lead humanity to Jesus, to reveal the beauty of the Savior, and to embody the heart of Christ like Isaiah.

21

The Prophet Commissioned

Living as God's Voice, Vessel, and
Ambassador in the Earth

INTRODUCTION: THE FINAL FORMATION OF A FULLY PREPARED PROPHET

Every chapter of this book has been a step—
a shaping, a chiseling, a refining, a deepening.
A prophet is not born in a moment but formed through a lifetime.

They are shaped by intimacy (like Enoch),
broken by burden (like Jeremiah),
steadied by endurance,
purified through crushing,
guided by discernment,
and anchored in Christ (like Isaiah).

Now, in this last chapter, we gather every lesson, every dimension, every refinement and prepare the prophet to step into divine commissioning—

not simply to operate in gifting,
but to live as God's representative,
His voice,
His vessel,
His ambassador,
His friend,
and His reflection in the earth.

This chapter is the prophetic mantle placed on the shoulders of the prepared prophet.

1. THE COMMISSIONING BEGINS WITH IDENTITY

Before a prophet can be commissioned, they must fully embrace who they are in God's Kingdom. Identity precedes assignment.

A prepared prophet knows:

- they are chosen,
- they are called,
- they are set apart,
- they are anointed,
- they are covered,
- they are equipped,
- they are responsible,
- they are accountable,
- they are protected,
- they are loved.

Prophets who lack identity seek validation.
Prophets who possess identity seek obedience.

Identity stabilizes the prophet and prevents insecurity from corrupting the calling.

2. COMMISSIONING REQUIRES FULL SURRENDER

Before God sends a prophet, He requires surrender—not partial, not occasional, not conditional, but total. Total surrender means:

- God has permission to redirect your life,
- God can interrupt your plans,
- God can use you in inconvenient seasons,
- God can ask for hard obedience,
- God can adjust your relationships,
- God can prune your environment,
- God can silence you,
- God can send you.

Prophets must surrender not only their will but their reputation, comfort, expectations, and timelines.

True prophetic power flows from surrender, not ambition.

3. THE COMMISSIONING ESTABLISHES DIVINE AUTHORITY

A prophet is not self-appointed.
They are God-appointed.

Divine commissioning gives the prophet:

- spiritual authority,
- revelation authority,
- interpretive authority,
- intercessory authority,
- territorial authority,
- atmospheric authority.

This authority is not loud—it is heavy.
Not flashy—it is weighty.
Not arrogant—it is humble.

The prophet carries Heaven's backing when Heaven has commissioned them.

4. THE PROPHET IS COMMISSIONED AS A VOICE OF TRUTH

The prepared prophet must be committed to truth—not popular truth, convenient truth, or culturally acceptable truth, but God's truth.

Truth that confronts darkness,
truth that cuts through deception,
truth that stands against corruption,
truth that reveals Christ,
truth that calls for repentance,
truth that brings healing.

Truth is not an opinion—it is a Person.
The prophet speaks truth because they walk with Truth Himself.

5. THE PROPHET IS COMMISSIONED AS A VESSEL OF LOVE

Prophets must carry the heart of God in equal measure to the voice of God. Without love, prophecy becomes sharp without being surgical, strong without being redemptive, and accurate without being healing.

Love softens delivery.
Love corrects with compassion.
Love restores the broken.
Love hosts the presence of God.
Love keeps the prophet grounded, tender, and safe.

A prophet without love becomes a hammer.
A prophet with love becomes a healer.

6. THE PROPHET IS COMMISSIONED AS A GUARDIAN OF HOLINESS

Prophets stand as watchmen of purity in a polluted world. They protect:

- holiness in the church,
- holiness in leadership,
- holiness in worship,
- holiness in doctrine,
- holiness in culture,
- holiness in their own life.

Holiness is not legalism—
it is alignment with God's nature.

The prophet is commissioned to guard the sacred.

7. THE PROPHET IS COMMISSIONED AS A CARRIER OF GOD'S PRESENCE

Prophets do not simply speak for God—they carry Him. The presence of God rests upon the prophet's life in such a way that:

- atmospheres shift when they enter a room,
- hidden things surface,
- darkness grows uncomfortable,
- hearts soften,
- captives sense freedom,
- and believers feel strengthened.

The prophet becomes a mobile sanctuary—
a living place of encounter.

8. THE PROPHET IS COMMISSIONED AS AN INTERCESSOR

God does not trust prophets who do not pray.
Intercession is the prophet's first form of ministry.

A commissioned prophet:

- prays for leaders,
- prays for nations,
- prays for the church,
- prays for families,
- prays for the broken,
- prays for the lost,
- prays for their own heart.

Intercession is the unseen labor that fuels visible authority.
The deeper the intercession, the farther the prophetic reach.

9. THE PROPHET IS COMMISSIONED AS A PROTECTOR OF GOD'S PEOPLE

Prophets are spiritual guardians who:

- warn of danger,
- expose deception,
- reveal hidden strategies,
- identify demonic traps,
- break spiritual attacks,
- and shield the vulnerable.

Protection is not always gentle.
Sometimes it is loud.
Sometimes it is urgent.
Sometimes it is confrontational.

But it is always motivated by love and obedience.

10. THE PROPHET IS COMMISSIONED INTO LIFELONG LEARNING

The prophetic mantle grows heavier through time. The prophet must remain teachable throughout their entire life. A commissioned prophet must commit to:

- studying Scripture deeply,
- learning the ways of the Spirit,
- understanding prophetic patterns,
- responding to correction,
- seeking mentorship,
- maturing emotionally,
- refining discernment continuously.

A teachable prophet becomes a trustworthy prophet.

11. COMMISSIONING INCLUDES THE MANTLE OF RESPONSIBILITY

The prophet must carry their calling with the utmost seriousness. Prophetic irresponsibility can:

- mislead people,
- wound hearts,
- distort doctrine,
- cause spiritual confusion,
- or misrepresent God.

Thus, the commissioned prophet carries responsibility like:

- a soldier carries a weapon,
- a surgeon carries a scalpel,
- a pilot carries a cockpit,
- a priest carries the holy things.

Responsibility is weight—but holy weight.

12. THE PROPHET IS COMMISSIONED WITH COURAGE

Prophetic calling requires courage because prophets often:

- stand against the majority,
- speak unpopular messages,
- challenge ungodly systems,
- confront hidden sin,
- expose demonic schemes,

- and call people to repentance.

Cowardice is incompatible with the prophetic mantle.
Courage does not mean fearlessness; it means obedience despite fear.

The commissioned prophet stands firm.

13. COMMISSIONING DEMANDS EMOTIONAL BALANCE

Prophets must manage:

- passion,
- clarity,
- sensitivity,
- compassion,
- righteous anger,
- inner tension.

Emotional imbalance distorts revelation, twists motives, and damages relationships.
A commissioned prophet must steward their emotions carefully so they can deliver God's word accurately.

14. THE PROPHET IS COMMISSIONED TO SERVE, NOT RULE

Prophets are not kings.
They are not spiritual dictators.
They are not untouchable elites.

They are servants—chosen to:

- wash feet,
- lift burdens,
- encourage the weary,
- strengthen leaders,
- serve the Body,
- and love people.

Great prophets are humble servants.
Their greatness is measured in compassion, not control.

15. THE PROPHET IS COMMISSIONED TO FINISH THEIR RACE WELL

The prophet's commissioning is not merely for the present—it is for the entire lifespan. God calls the prophet to finish well:

- with integrity,
- with purity,
- with humility,
- with consistency,
- with passion,
- with Christ at the center.

Finishing well is the prophet's final prophecy.

A prophet who ends faithfully leaves a legacy that outlives their words.

CONCLUSION: THE PROPHET STEPS INTO THEIR KINGDOM ASSIGNMENT

With this final chapter, the prophet stands ready.
The crushing has shaped them.

The intimacy has anchored them.
The calling has matured them.
The tears of Jeremiah have softened them.
The walk of Enoch has drawn them closer.
The visions of Isaiah have centered them in Christ.
The endurance of the saints has steadied them.
The redemptive message of the Savior has captured their heart.

Now they stand—
not as a novice,
not as a wanderer,
not as a gifted voice without foundation,
but as a prepared prophet.

A prophet who is:

- surrendered,
- balanced,
- purified,
- refined,
- commissioned,
- protected,
- empowered,
- and established.

This is the prophet who carries God's heart into the earth.
This is the prophet who shifts atmospheres.
This is the prophet who strengthens the Church.
This is the prophet who confronts darkness.
This is the prophet who makes Christ known.
This is the prophet who endures until the end.
This is the prophet who walks with God.

The world does not simply need prophets—it needs prepared prophets.

And now, by the grace of God, by the power of the Spirit, and by the example of Scripture, you are one of them.

22

Epilogue

The Prophet Sent Forth

A prophet is not prepared merely to be formed—
they are prepared to be sent.

After all the reading, refining, praying, crying, surrendering, wrestling, and rising,
there comes a moment when God whispers,
"Now go."

Go and speak.
Go and serve.
Go and stand.
Go and intercede.
Go and shine.
Go and love.
Go and warn.
Go and build.
Go and heal.

Go and direct humanity to Christ.

Prophets do not go in their own strength.
They go in God's authority.
They go with God's presence resting on their shoulders.
They go armed with discernment, compassion, and holiness.
They go carrying the message of redemption, anchored in the Cross.

And although the world may misunderstand them, Heaven understands them completely.

The prophet steps forward not because they feel qualified but because they feel called. Not because they are fearless, but because they trust the One who goes before them. Not because they carry clarity about every step, but because they carry obedience in every step.

You are now equipped.
You are now strengthened.
You are now forged in fire.
You are now anchored in Christ.
You are now ready.

Go forth, Prepared Prophet,
for the Kingdom is waiting
for the voice God placed inside you.

Dr. Tony E. Medley Sr. is a visionary leader, teacher, and prophetic voice committed to equipping the Body of Christ for deeper intimacy with God, stronger spiritual maturity, and unwavering biblical integrity. With a ministry journey spanning decades, Dr. Medley has become known for his unique ability to bring clarity to complex spiritual truths while inspiring believers to rise into their God-given purpose.

A passionate communicator of Scripture, Dr. Medley's teachings emphasize holiness, prophetic purity, emotional health, and life-giving transformation through the power of Jesus Christ. His messages carry a rare blend of revelation, practicality, compassion, and spiritual authority—reflecting a life deeply shaped by prayer, consecration, and personal encounters with God.

Beyond the pulpit, Dr. Medley serves as a respected Christian counselor, author, and organizational leader. He has written numerous inspirational, theological, and devotional works designed to strengthen faith, restore hope, and guide believers toward Christ-centered living. His writing style is marked by depth, clarity, and a strong desire to see God's people walking in truth, purpose, and prophetic sensitivity.

Dr. Medley is also an educator and founder of transformative Christian training initiatives dedicated to developing emerging leaders, ministers, and prophetic voices. His multi-dimensional approach—combining biblical scholarship, pastoral care, leadership development, and prophetic insight—has impacted individuals, churches, and communities across the nation.

Across every assignment, Dr. Medley's mission remains unwavering: to glorify Jesus Christ, strengthen the Church, and prepare a generation of believers to hear God clearly, walk with Him deeply, and serve Him faithfully.

Dr. Tony E. Medley Sr. resides in Georgia, where he continues his work of writing, teaching, mentoring, and proclaiming the message of Christ with passion, excellence, and unwavering devotion.